WORLD

AWAKENING

WORLD

AWAKENING

Donald R. Howard, Ph.D.

New Leaf Press
P.O. BOX 311, GREEN FOREST, AR 72638

First Edition
1988

Library of Congress Catalog Number: 88-62244
ISBN: 0-89221-162-8

Dedicated to
encourage Bible-believing Christians
to keep the faith
during these perilous times
by giving them specific evidence
of God's marvelous workings
in the world today.

Table of Contents

PERSPECTIVE

You are living in the greatest period in the history of the world. This is the most perplexing and yet the most exciting and rewarding time to be alive. The future of supercomputers, fiber optics, laser technology, and robotics is fast becoming the present. As mankind approaches the end of another millennium, all history--past, present, and future--is being brought into focus.

Some experts tell us the world is getting worse and that we are living in "perilous times"--headed for imminent chaos and doom. Others tell us we may be in the middle of the greatest Divine "Harvest Time" of God-consciousness and redemption in the history of mankind.

There is a possibility that neither is true. Yet, there is more of a probability that *both* are true. Two parallel themes in the Bible seem to indicate "last days" activities that appear to be mutually exclusive. These two themes read like an apparent contradiction. Notice:

"... in the *last days* perilous times shall come."
II Timothy 3:1

> ". . . in the *last days* . . . I will pour out of my Spirit upon all flesh . . ."
>
> Acts 2:17

Each context is obviously referring to the Church Age, that era of almost 2000 years that has passed since the death of Christ and until His return. Each context elaborates on either a negative or positive influence and the extent that visitation will have on people and culture. Each context also identifies the increased intensity with which it will impact people and culture in the "last" of the "last days." (The negative [II Timothy 3:1] influence of Western culture and the source of its degradation, as well as the cause and the only cure, are discussed in *TEEN TURMOIL*, the companion volume to this book.)

It is to the *growing, positive* influence of Acts 2:17 that this book addresses little known facts from history and contemporary times. Many of these facts were gleaned from this author's travels of more than ten times around the world, and from visits repeated over a decade to more than 75 countries of the world--with the growing conviction that *God is now intervening in history for one final, colossal time leading up to the Apocalypse of our Lord.*

1

WHERE IS GOD?

> ". . . in the last days, . . . I will pour out of my Spirit
> upon all flesh . . ." (Acts 2:17)

Today, according to the polls and experts, 96 percent of
all Americans believe in God and 62 percent believe Jesus
Christ is coming back.

But many are asking: "Where is God?" "Is He present
and active in human affairs today?" "Can we perceive His
presence and actions?"

If we heard about or witnessed God's actions today,
would we even recognize them? Would the news media report
on them?

Probably not. It is difficult, in *any* age, to discern God's
activities. This is partly because God's ways are not our ways.
We approach the supernatural aspects of God's activities
with our own ideas of how He should act. Man has always
been conditioned to want to *see* Him or be entertained by
some miracle He might perform on their behalf.

Part of this conditioning has been done by the mass
media. The truth of God's presence and activity is virtually

obscured by the popular media, giving the world a distorted view of reality.

The media focuses on the sensational, thus emphasizing the trivial, confusing, or exceptional situation. The media will give plenty of coverage to fallen church leaders, but will probably not mention that these leaders are in the "woodshed" and will say nothing of what God is really doing in the world.

The mass media reflects a secular and humanistic worldview. As such, the media is not merely neutral in matters relating to God or the Church, but has a definite anti-religious bias.

The media does not see God's hand in world affairs because God does not fit into their established and biased world-view. Misinformation, distortion, and concentration on trivial or sensational side issues of the Church by the media result in confusion and ignorance. The really important facts go unreported. (News that sells is often not "news" at all, and if it won't "sell," it's not "news.") The average Christian, therefore, is as much in the dark as the world in general when it comes to seeing and understanding *the most significant facts, trends, and events.*

While the modern mass media is to blame for events that relate to God's activities in the world going unreported, for the most part, this blindness is not a new phenomenon; it seems this has always been the case. Two thousand years ago, Jesus "was in the world, and the world was made by him, and the world knew him not" (John 1:10).

The God of Creation and Ruler of the Universe wrapped Himself in human flesh and walked on this planet for over 30 years. Yet, He went largely unrecognized. Then, "He came unto his own," that is, His own race, His own people, His own ethnic group, "and his own received him not" (verse 11).

Most of the people of Jesus' day missed out on the *greatest* of Divine interventions. They heard Him speak in the Temple and synagogues. Some even commented that "never man spake like this man." Yet, "his own received him not."

Periodically God has intervened in human history, and

in nearly every case, the people who were living in that time and place missed it. They were not aware of God's intervention. Future generations read about it in history.

In the days of Noah, God intervened and only eight believed and survived. The Exodus of Israel from Egypt was surrounded by miracles, yet the Egyptians and even many of the Israelites of that generation did not understand what God was doing. Throughout the Old Testament (especially the Psalms), the truth of God's intervention in the lives of His people is richly illustrated.

God has also intervened in other nations and in other periods of time. Following the Crucifixion of Jesus Christ, Jerusalem was destroyed and the Jews were scattered across the earth. The Christian Church was nearly extinguished as well; however, a remnant not only survived but, by God's grace and blessing, flourished.

In the Dark Ages, corruption and superstition again nearly destroyed the Church, but God intervened. A supernatural reformation transformed the entire Western culture.

History has many more illustrations of God's intervention in human affairs in modern times, but these interventions are more readily apparent in *retrospect*. People living at the time of these activities tend to be unaware of God's intervening. If God were to publish a *Heavenly Herald* and an angel were to deliver a copy to your mailbox each morning, you could read it at breakfast and say, "Hey, folks, look what God is doing today. WOW!" But that is not God's method. He does not condescend to curiosity or to man's human taste for the fascinating.

Since we are conditioned by contemporary culture to accept only those facts that the world system exonerates through the media, God's agenda is usually missed--even by the Church.

Then, is it possible to know what God is doing today? We may perceive what God is doing in our local church, our denomination, our town, and so forth; but we tend not to get the **BIG PICTURE.** We tend to lack essential information of what may be happening outside our sphere of experience.

One does not have to be a prophet or have the gift of prophecy to know that if you identify the significant events from history and you see significant influences and trends from the past moving into the present, you can then often project these influences and trends into the future.

FIRST: To understand what God is doing we must have a reasonable understanding of *history*. By seeing how God worked in the past, we can often interpret what He is doing now. Since His principles do not change, we can chart trends and predict the future with a relative degree of accuracy. The key concepts we must understand are:

    1. Significant events.
    2. Trends.

SECOND: Understanding of what God is doing often comes from facts and information about the contemporary world that are not always at our disposal. God is not just working in our local church; His work is universal, and information regarding this work may not always be accessible to us. Without seeing the BIG PICTURE, it is difficult to see that it is in fact GOD. The universal hand of God is seldom sensational and rarely, if ever, attracts the media.

THIRD: To perceive the hand of God, we must understand *Bible principles*. As we move into what most Bible scholars refer to as the "end times," we are made aware of an enormous volume of Biblical passages that are now of extreme significance. These Biblical passages are more than interesting. They are absolutely critical in our understanding and application of truth for *today* and for the immediate future.

When we study these facts of history, as well as contemporary facts and information, and gather and compare Scriptural principles with current international information and historical trends, the Holy Spirit guides us into truth and gives us an "understanding of the times," allowing us to *see the reality* of "end-time" events.

As we apply this "understanding of the times," we can understand not only what God is doing today, but how to be *involved in it*--to motivate ourselves and others to necessary

Christian action and to help focus on the most critical responsibilities for life and soul for these "last days."

In order to clearly focus on this truth and task, it is important to examine the period from about 1970 through the end of the twentieth century. This 30-year period (one generation) is without a doubt a most important period in our lifetime. It may even be the most significant period in the history of the world!

Don't "miss out" on what GOD IS DOING!

IS GOD INTERVENING?

A.D. 2000

1970   1975   1980   1985   1990   1995

2

THE LAST GENERATION

"Things fall apart; the center cannot hold.
Mere anarchy is loosed upon the world."
William Butler Yeats

In the *TIME* magazine cover article "1968: The Year That Shaped a Generation," Lance Morrow wrote, "Like a knife blade, the year (1968) severed past from future."

The events of 1968 acted as a catalyst in establishing new ways, ideas, and values for that generation. In addition, 1968 was a microcosm, a capsule preview, of events to come in the next three decades. As Morrow says, "Nineteen sixty-eight had the vibrations of earthquakes about it. America shuddered. History cracked open: bats came flapping out dark surprises. American culture and politics ventured into dangerous and experimental regions."

The year was both tragic and hopeful--bloody, astonishing, ecstatic, energized. Some characters in this "drama" were absurd, others inspiring; some self-destructive, others noble; some chaotic, others spiritually fulfilling.

In the confusing collision of old and new, a "counter-culture" was created. It mocked the old values (the continuity of history and tradition) and took a conceited focus on its own desires, needs, and wants. They sang, "This is the dawning of the age of Aquarius," as well as, "Where have you gone, Joe DiMaggio?"

A summary of events as they occurred in 1968 shows the year as a microcosm for the rest of the century, with the media mixing the reporting of significant events alongside trivial ones, giving both equality in the minds of the audiences.

JANUARY--America's reputation as a world power is eroded when North Korea captures the U.S.S. *Pueblo* and as the Viet Cong launches its Tet offensive.

FEBRUARY--Three black students are killed when disturbances erupt as the students try to desegregate a South Carolina bowling alley. Black rage was the theme of Eldridge Cleaver's new book, *Soul On Ice.*

MARCH--Traditional, established political party structures become vulnerable as political "bosses" lose their influence. Senator Eugene McCarthy does well in primaries, and President Lyndon Johnson announces he will not run again for the Presidency.

APRIL--Rampant violence occurs. Martin Luther King is assassinated; racial riots break out in several cities, including the nation's capital (where federal troops are called up). Federal troops are also sent to Chicago to stop racial violence. Student demonstrations close the campus of Columbia University.

MAY--Student unrest sweeps across the U.S. and overseas. Students in Paris riot, using slingshots against police. The riots grow into paralyzing strikes by workers and threaten the collapse of the French government.

JUNE--An unbelieving country is notified that Robert Kennedy (the second leader in two months and the second Kennedy) is assassinated. Overseas, the same day, violent Arab protests take place in Israeli-occupied territory.

JULY--Terrorists hijack a commercial airliner over Italy. Meanwhile, the civil war between Biafra and Nigeria continues with starvation and killings mounting to unprecedented numbers.

AUGUST--Conflict between nations is prominent. In addition, skirmishes break out between North and South Korea, North and South Viet Nam, Israel and Egypt, and Israel and Jordan. A number of coups and attempted coups occur. Czechoslovakia is invaded by tanks and troops from Russia and other Communist neighbors. Yet, this event is obscured by events in the U.S. where terrible violence erupts between police and demonstrators at the Democratic Convention in Chicago.

SEPTEMBER--Nations in Africa seek and find independence from colonial rule, some with better results than others. Swaziland becomes independent of Great Britain, while political turmoil continues in Rhodesia.

OCTOBER--More traditions and perceptions are smashed as the summer Olympic games in Mexico are marred by an estimated 300 to 500 student and civilian casualties after soldiers open fire on a crowd of some 10,000. The other graphic reminder of the games is the picture of two black American athletes with upraised clenched fist in the "black power" salute.

NOVEMBER--Chemical poison and pollution are beginning to alarm scientists. Several of the Great Lakes are, for all practical purposes, already "dead." An earlier test of biological weapons killed 500 sheep in Utah, and a B-52 bomber carrying nuclear weapons crashed in Greenland.

DECEMBER--The U.S.S.R. has launched some ten spacecrafts during the year; the U.S., eleven. The year ends on a lovely and optimistic note as Apollo 8 astronauts orbit the moon and see the distant earth in serene beauty.

The media perception communicates that 1968 has a distinct and separate identity and stands apart from the rest of the '60s. However, the fact is, 1968 was not a separate year at all. It was an extension of trends which began earlier and the pattern of events to follow--many of which simply climaxed in 1968. Frightening and negative influences seemed to emphasize decline, and believers were stimulated to quote II Chronicles 7:14: "If my people, which are called by my name, shall humble themselves, and pray, and seek my face, and turn from their wicked ways; then will I hear from heaven, and will forgive their sin, and will heal their land."

It was 1968 that motivated American Christians to seek God's will regarding their world, their faith, and their nation. It was 1968 that helped American Christians get off the pew and get busy.

How was God preparing America, the Church, and the world for what could be the last great movement of God during this last generation of the twentieth century?

The events of 1968 demonstrated that the old order was shaken. *How would God intervene?* Does God intervene through events, natural or man-made disasters, wars, trends, buildings, machines, or inventions? The Scripture illustrates that God intervenes through *His people:* a **REMNANT!**

An active spiritual awakening and renewal is often begun through just a handful of people. Key people are led by God through significant events in their times. These key people are the ones who are actively involved in *God's Word* and a movement of *righteousness*.

Following the chaos and darkness of the 60's (which had been building since World War II), a remnant of people and programs surfaced for the 1970's and 1980's and into the 1990's-- something extremely significant for the end of this century and millennium.

To look back now, after nearly two decades (to around 1970), is to recognize the significance of key people and the major movements they began. It could very well be that they (and not the counterculture influence of 1968) represent the *most significant and far-reaching influences* in the history of the West.

Documenting these people and their achievements is not necessarily to endorse them nor any particular aspect of their given ministries. Nor can this book be conclusive in listing all of this "remnant" of God's people and programs. If someone is inadvertently left out of the list, it does not mean there is a question about his ministry.

Conversely, not everyone listed may have continued his walk with God. Later sin or reproach may cloud the significance that person or organization has today.

Conscientious believers must acknowledge the need to "let God be God." That is, God uses people with whom we may not agree. God uses *all* of us, not *because* of us but *in spite* of us.

3

THE MOST SIGNIFICANT YEAR OF THE CENTURY: 1970

"Amazing grace! How sweet the sound that
saved a wretch like me."

John Newton

Drugs, sexual permissiveness, rebellion, and self-destruction seemed to be by-products of youth during the late 60's. But God began to move in power and redemption. "Hippies" were saved from obvious sin and their conversions were dramatic. (Incidentally, many of these "Jesus freaks" have long since cleaned up, cut their hair, and bought three-piece Ivy League suits. Some of them have even become pastors and have built conservative, Bible-believing churches.)

There were events that took place in the 60's which had equal significance to anything the media reported, but because the events were contrary to the media's bias or worldview, the events went largely unreported. Because they *went unreported* by the media, many people considered these events as having little or no significance. These events were spontaneous and took place in various places simultaneously. God was instrumental in the outpouring of His Spirit. But men from this remnant were His agents:

In the 1960's:

David Wilkerson and *Teen Challenge* con-founded media experts who said drug addiction had no cure. *Life* magazine showed conversions to Christ experienced through the *Teen Challenge* programs delivered from drugs.

On the West Coast, *Campus Crusade for Christ* leaders, *Dick Day* and *Josh McDowell*, began working with alienated youth.

Hal Lindsey and associates started Salt and Light Company for "Jesus people" discipleship.

In Chicago, *David Mains* began a church in a Teamsters Union hall and ministered to the counterculture; while in nearby Wheaton, Illinois, *Sam Wolgemuth* and *Jay Kesler* changed *Youth for Christ* from a rally-type church service into an aggressive para-church organization that presented Christ directly to rebellious kids, right in the high schools. Another work, *Young Life,* exploded on the scene with similar success.

In September 1966, *Jack Hyles,* pastor of the First Baptist Church of Hammond, Indiana, became burdened for America. He took a map of the United States to his basement, spread it out, got down on his knees, fell over that map, and began to fast and pray for America. The Lord led Dr. Hyles into a new ministry, to go out and be a "preacher to preachers." In the years following that experience, he has probably spoken to more pastors face to face than any preacher during the Church Age.

Christ for the Nations was founded in 1967 and began a Bible institute in 1970.

Tom Skinner, a young black militant and Harlem gang leader, was converted about this same time and started an evangelistic ministry with a special focus on black military and youth gangs.

Evangelism Explosion, started by *James Kennedy,* pastor of the Coral Ridge Presbyterian Church in Florida, was introduced and put into churches across the country through a *Gospel Films* documentary entitled *Like a Mighty Army.* Dr. Kennedy's Evangelism Explosion training for pastors has revolutionized the evangelism outreach ministries of literally thousands of churches.

Jack Van Impe, David Wilkerson, and *Billy Graham* were still conducting what were almost becoming rare: citywide evangelistic crusades. Television would soon be a means to reach the masses.

The 1960's also saw the greatest decline of mainline (liberal) Protestant denominations, as between three to five million members dropped from mainline denomination church rolls.

Just as the year 1968 seemed to predict the explosion of disorder and destruction of the 1970's, so did the decade of the 60's anticipate what God would do for the Church in the period to follow.

What was happening across America in the 60's was only a prophetic glimpse of the explosion to follow. If 1968 was the watershed year for what happened in our culture, then 1970 has to be the significant year of events for Christians:

In 1970--a young man wrote a best-selling book that challenged almost everything Benjamin Spock had taught about child rearing. *Dare to Discipline* by James Dobson sold over a million copies. He has since written eight other books (some have sold over four million copies) and founded a network, nationwide ministry, *Focus on the Family,* which directly confronts "anti-family" secular influences.

In 1970--the Christian school movement began to explode. *Accelerated Christian Education* opened its first school (in Texas), with 43 students.

Since then A.C.E. has grown to over 7000 schools in more than 90 countries, directly out of the God-given vision to *do something* (in obedience to Scripture) because of the moral and spiritual crises in our public schools.

In 1970--a pastor in San Diego, California, organized the first Unified Christian School district. *Pastor Tim LaHaye* also founded a Bible college. He and his wife, Beverly, began conducting *Family Life Seminars.* Tim and Bev LaHaye's books are widely read, and Tim LaHaye probably has more books on the desks of pastors than any other contemporary writer. He has helped to establish three major conservative political action organizations:

Council for National Policy,
Moral Majority, and
American Coalition for Traditional Values.

In 1970--a young man rented a room in a Garland, Texas bank building, where about 40 people came to hear him speak. *Bill Gothard* and his *Institute in Basic Youth Conflicts* was born. Ten years later, he had a nationwide ministry to hundreds of thousands of lay people and pastors.

In 1970--a young evangelist had a vision for a worldwide ministry of bringing people to Christ. His preaching was powerful and God used him to win souls. *Jimmy Swaggart* became the most influential evangelist in history, reaching hundreds of millions through crusades and television.

At the time of his well-publicized moral sin in 1988, Jimmy Swaggart was watched in more TV households worldwide than any other preacher. Some 70 percent of the homes in Central and South America, and millions more in Africa and other countries, watched his TV program an average of three times weekly.

In 1970--*Francis Schaeffer,* a prophetic philosopher-theologian, lectured on the theme of

"The Christian and Culture" and began a vast work which established him as one of the greatest Christian apologists of this century. Dr. Schaeffer stirred our "memory of absolutes."

In 1970--*Pat Robertson,* a young businessman, purchased a defunct television station for about $70 cash and put it on the air. Within a few years there were other stations, which then grew into the *CBN Network* (a cable TV network now worth nearly a half-billion dollars). CBN is said by the liberal secular press to have more influence than the nine largest newspapers in America combined. CBN is watched in over 34 million homes each week.

In 1970--*Jerry Falwell* completed preparations for the start of Liberty Baptist College the following September. Dr. Falwell later received national prominence as a church leader with the *Moral Majority* and the *Council for National Policy* as well as the *Super Conference* for pastors and church leaders. He also started a national television ministry, *The Old-Time Gospel Hour,* which reaches millions of Americans.

In 1970--there were about 150,000 *evangelical and Bible-believing churches* in America. They began to explode until today--because of the growth of Bible study groups and store-front churches--that number may have doubled. Current estimates range from 225,000 to over a quarter million, though the number could even approach 300,000 (doubling in 18 years).

In 1971--David Gibbs organized the Gibbs-Craze Law Firm in Cleveland, Ohio. In 1976 they established the Christian Law Association. Dr. Gibbs has been identified by Dr. Jack Hyles as the "Christian Legal Messiah" of this generation. His success in defending Christian schools and churches is overshadowed only by his Christian Legal Seminars, which reintroduce Biblical principles into our legal system.

In retrospect, it appears that 1970 was an *extremely significant* year--perhaps the most significant year of this century. In answer to corporate and individual prayers, God began to intervene in contemporary events *through His people.*

In 1942 the Committee for the Evangelization of the Greeks was established. In 1946 Spiros Zodhiates became Executive Secretary. In 1970-71 the organization changed its name to American Mission to the Greeks (A.M.G.) and greatly expanded its ministry. Radio stations were acquired, publications were established, hospitals and clinics were enlarged--especially in the United States and Greece. In 1976 the name was again changed--this time to Advancing the Ministries of the Gospel (A.M.G.). This time the organization began reaching into most of the free world.

In the next few years, others were called of God to address critical needs of our society and the Christian church. Some of these may have used different styles or methods than you or I may have used. Their expressions of worship or ministry may likewise have been different, and we may not necessarily endorse them or every aspect of their ministry.

In the past such differences created division and opposing factions. But remarkably, in the 1970s more believers began to work and worship together. Believers began to see that, instead of attacking each other's doctrinal differences, musical styles, or worship approaches, Christians needed to unite to combat more common and pervasive foes of the faith: abortion, humanism, atheism, pornography, godless values, and immorality.

Curiously, the same mass media that brought some of these evils into our living rooms were also being used to bring God's Word to the world: Christian television, radio, magazines, and books exploded in the 1970s. The *700 Club, PTL Club, Jimmy Swaggart Ministries,* Charles Stanley's daily *In Touch,* Robert Schuler's *Hour of Power,* Oral Roberts, Rex Humbard, Jerry Falwell's *Old-Time Gospel Hours,* Richard DeHaan's *Day of Discovery* were just a few of the scores of programs that touched millions of hearts and lives.

For the first time, Christian books began to outsell secular titles. *Newsweek* magazine described the situation, noting that a "best seller" was a book that sold at least 50,000 copies and that if the *New York Times* and other publishers of "best-seller" lists were to list all the best-selling books, the majority would be Christian titles. The *New York Times* did make occasional exceptions by listing the best-selling titles by *Billy Graham, Catherine Marshall,* and *Charles Colson.*

Secular publishers began offering Christian titles in paperback racks in airports, drugstores, and discount chains. *The Cross and the Switchblade, The Late Great Planet Earth,* and *Christy* brought Christian testimony, Biblical prophecy, and drama into the hands of multiplied millions. In addition to books, *U.S. News and World Report* indicates that contemporary Christian music (which came on the scene in 1970-71) now outsells jazz and classical recordings.

Until 1970 Bible bookstores were somewhat unique to some large cities. Then *Christian bookstores* began springing up, many right in some of the larger downtown churches. Bible bookstores are now in almost every city and many small towns. Over 7000 Bible bookstores are selling over a billion dollars worth of Christian literature and products each year.

The rest of the 70's built on this supernatural surge of God's intervention which took place in 1970.

In 1971 *Charles Colson* was in the White House on President Nixon's staff. In 1974 he was in the "jailhouse." The secular media made much of Colson's "foxhole conversion," but his faith proved real. When released from prison, Colson founded *Prison Fellowship,* which has grown to be an effective para-church ministry in America and some 35 other countries. Chuck Colson introduced the reality of the expression "born again" to exclusive Washington, D.C., society and political circles.

In 1971 *Rochunga Pudaite* founded *Bibles for the World.* Dr. Pudaite, who was the grandson of a Northeast India headhunter, wanted to give to the world the Book that set his people free. He founded *Bibles for the World* with the goal to mail a Bible or

New Testament, in the native language of the people, to the home of every family listed in telephone directories around the world. He plans to achieve his "billion Bible dream" by the year 2000.

In 1971 *Charles Stanley* became the senior pastor of the great First Baptist Church of Atlanta, Georgia. This began a major fundamental movement in the influential church. Dr. Stanley began a radio ministry that expanded across the U.S., then overseas. His *In Touch* radio and cassette tape ministries are today worldwide.

In 1971 *Bill Bright* organized *Explo '72.* His goal was to bring together some 80,000 students from "hippie-infested" university campuses for the study of evangelism and Christian discipleship. This was followed in 1975 with the first of the *Campus Crusade* "Here's Life, America" citywide campaigns. The "I Found It" slogans appeared on billboards worldwide. Soon billboards began to display all kinds of advertisements regarding Christian ministries and churches. The same was true of bumper stickers.

Commentator *Paul Harvey* helps promote the bumper sticker fad. Many of the stickers are whimsical, even trite; but even a message such as "Honk if you love Jesus," seen all over the country, shows a growing interest in the "born again" phenomenon.

During the 70's and 80's, billboards and bumper stickers all across America advertised churches, Christian schools, and Gospel services on an unprecedented scale. (Some huge billboards placed in front yards of homes heralded the Gospel and salvation.) But the advertising was not limited to billboards and bumper stickers. My wife, Esther, opened a carton of Cumberland Valley, Grade A, eggs. Inside the lid was a printed message: "For by grace are ye saved through faith; and that not of yourselves: it is the gift of God: not of works, lest any man should boast" (Ephesians 2:8, 9). (A pastor who also saw it quipped, "And that ain't no yoke!")

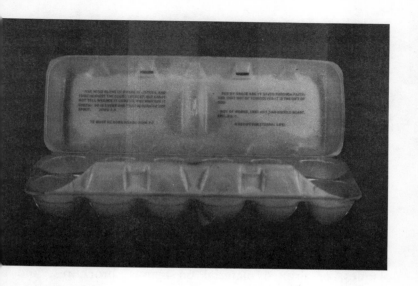

In 1970-71 there were only a handful of *Christian radio stations* in America. Most were located in large cities and were affiliated with local organizations, such as Moody Bible Institute's WMBI Chicago. A number of new broadcast missionaries trusted God, and today there are over 1300 radio stations with a Christian format and over 200 television stations with a Christian format. There are also more than a dozen Christian radio and television *networks*. This type and volume of program production and broadcasting is only possible when there is a large enough audience or number of citizens willing to finance it.

In 1970-71 you could eat in most any restaurant in the country and not see anyone *saying grace in public* before the meal. Now it is rare to eat a meal and *not* see several individuals or families saying grace. In fact, *Weekend Magazine* (January 1, 1987) reported from a survey that over *half* of the homes with children in America say grace at mealtime.

Christians did not promote their faith and identify with Christianity in their businesses in 1970-71. (It probably would have hurt their business to emphasize to their customers that they were believers.) That has changed. We walked into a Fresno restaurant in 1985 where the Christian fish symbol:

was prominently placed on the front door. Elsewhere we find similar marks of identification, including signs, Scriptural plaques, or printed material on menus, brochures, and so forth.

One of our staff members purchased from the produce counter of his local supermarket a bag of carrots with the Christian identification symbol in the corner:

One Dallas firm has even published a complete directory of Christian businesses for the Dallas/Fort Worth Metroplex.

A pastor in Oklahoma brought me an invoice with a prominent Christian symbol from a local termite exterminator:

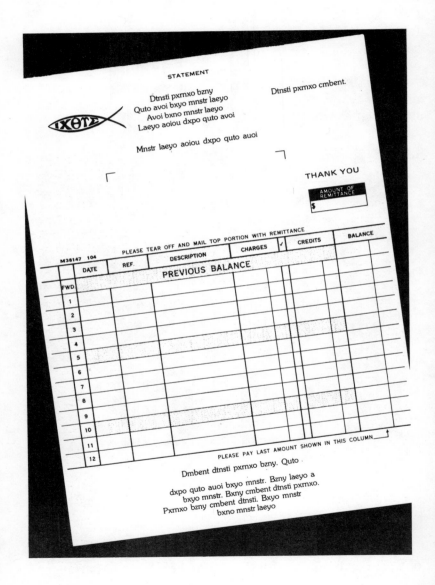

STATEMENT

Dtnsti pxrnxo bzny
Quto avoi bxyo mnstr laeyo
Avoi bxno mnstr laeyo
Laeyo aoiou dxpo quto avoi

Dtnsti pxrnxo cmbent.

Mnstr laeyo aoiou dxpo quto auoi

THANK YOU

AMOUNT OF
REMITTANCE

$

PLEASE TEAR OFF AND MAIL TOP PORTION WITH REMITTANCE

M38147 104

	DATE	REF.	DESCRIPTION	CHARGES	✓	CREDITS	BALANCE
			PREVIOUS BALANCE				
FWD.							
1							
2							
3							
4							
5							
6							
7							
8							
9							
10							
11							
12							

PLEASE PAY LAST AMOUNT SHOWN IN THIS COLUMN

Dmbent dtnsti pxrnxo bzny. Quto
dxpo quto auoi bxyo mnstr. Bzny laeyo a
bxyo mnstr. Bxny cmbent dtnsti pxrnxo.
Pxrnxo bzny cmbent dtnsti. Bxyo mnstr
bxno mnstr laeyo

A number of Christian businessmen and families even have a Scripture verse at the top of their checks.

What began to happen in 1970 foreshadowed events to come. More and more Christians are involved in politics. Governors and congressmen acknowledge their Christian faith. In fact, the last three Presidents have all claimed to have had a born-again experience. Many politicians are more open about their faith and testimony.

Bob Moreland, of Georgia, and other Christian politicians use Scripture and statements about their faith and testimonies in their political brochures.

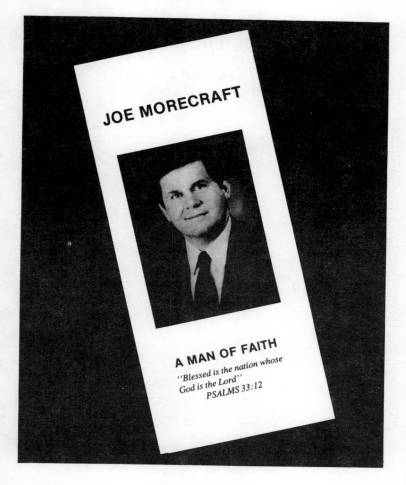

JOE MORECRAFT

A MAN OF FAITH

"Blessed is the nation whose God is the Lord"
PSALMS 33:12

Governor Guy Hunt of Alabama is pastor of two Baptist churches where he preaches on weekends. As a minister of the Gospel, he has even performed marriages in the governor's mansion.

There are now Praise the Lord toys on the market. These dolls (Faith, Love, Hope, and Joy) don't say "Mama." They say "Jesus loves me," sing Gospel songs, and recite Bible verses. This is yet another unusual twist to this growing phenomenon.

In 1970, Christians were not very visible or vocal. Today, they are both.

> **Without question, 1970 is the most significant year of the century. During 1970, TRENDS started that are impacting the WORLD.**

4

THE MOST
SIGNIFICANT TRENDS

During the summer of 1986, a Los Angeles attorney visited my office. We were discussing a school tax problem in California. In the course of our conversation, the lawyer shared his faith. It somewhat caught me off guard because I understood him to be a member of a traditionally liberal mainline denomination.

"You're a member of the Congregational Church?" I asked.

"Yes," he replied.

"But how can you function in such a liberal denomination?"

He answered, "Last fall we had a revival in our church. The pastor got saved, and so did most of the members."

This Los Angeles attorney also said, "The Headquarters Church on Park Street, in Boston, also had a revival. They publish the house organ for the denomination." With a sparkle in his eyes, he added, "You should read the literature that's published there now!"

During our fall Christian Educators' Convention tour,

the van driver was taking us from the hotel back to the airport. During the drive, I learned he was a Roman Catholic. "I wonder, if you were to die, would you know for sure that you'd go to Heaven?" I asked him.

"I sure would!" he replied, not missing a beat.

"How would you know for sure?" I asked.

"Because Jesus is my Savior and my sins are forgiven," the young man told me.

"Where did you learn that?" I wondered.

At first he said nothing, then muttered, "I can't tell you."

"You mean it's some kind of a secret?"

"Uh . . . yeah, something like that," he said.

After some more questions and prompting, the driver explained what had happened. "Last summer a priest conducted a four-day retreat in the mountains and I was there." He told us how the priest first took each one attending down the "Roman's Road" and led each one to Christ. He then showed them how to have assurance of forgiveness.

"He showed us how to read the Bible and study it in order to grow spiritually," the driver said. "He showed us the great doctrine of the faith and taught us how to share our faith and lead others to Christ. When the priest finished the retreat, he closed his Bible and said, 'Now don't tell anyone who told you.' "

Today, over seven million Roman Catholics in America profess to be born again. A former Roman Catholic recently gave this testimony while at the Accelerated Christian Education facility in Lewisville, Texas:

> I was raised in a Catholic church. We had a Bible in our home, but we never read it because the church discouraged that kind of thing. When I was in college, I began to search for truth, and in my readings I included the Bible. Jesus Christ walked out of the pages of the Bible and into my life. I became radically different.
>
> Then as the Lord would have it, I was doing my student teaching in a school right in my own home

town. I was able to live at home and to spend my time reading and consuming the Bible. My parents went to the priest, and he told them I shouldn't be reading the Bible because it was something only priests could interpret.

I became very bitter and angry at the Catholic Church. I remember having arguments with my parents about the statues. (I am Italian, and many Italian homes have a little place for their statues.) My mom was very ill at one point and needed surgery. People from the church came to visit her and gave her little statues to put in her hospital room. I came in and removed them all, and then we anointed her with oil and prayed. The Lord intervened in her behalf.

Later, my mom started going to a prayer meeting at the Catholic church. When she tried to tell me about it, I did not even want to listen. But then I noticed that she became alive. I saw her staying up late to read the Bible. She began asking me questions and having discussions with me about the Bible.

I learned that the priests in the church where I was raised had gotten saved, and there was a renewal movement. They had gone to retreats where born-again priests had led them to Christ. I went to a service where the Gospel was preached; the sermon was about living the Christian life, and the people were given an opportunity to receive Christ as their Savior. Incredible!

An article on the front page of the *Washington Post* (1986) headlined, "The Christians Are Coming." *TIME, NEWSWEEK,* and *U.S. News and World Report* have also given national prominence to the growing Christian movement.

Elmer Towns, an authority on trends among Bible-believing Christians, reports that in 1968 there were 97 Sunday schools in America with an average of over 1000 in attendance. Eighteen years later (in 1986) there were over 8160 Sunday schools with over 1000 in attendance.

Newspapers and magazines report how Christians have become politically organized, have demanded school curriculum changes, and have become activists on moral issues:

> In Virginia Beach, Virginia, Christians forced doctors to stop performing abortions.

> In San Antonio, Texas, sexually oriented cable TV channels were protested by local Christians.

> In a number of states, Christians have fought for and won the right to home school their children or to open their own Christian schools.

> In Lexington, Kentucky, two of the largest tobacco warehouses were closed.

The tobacco industry has been hard hit recently, as evidence of Bible principles affecting culture. "No smoking" sections in restaurants and public buildings, and even the workplace, have been won. Hotels even offer non-smoking rooms on non-smoking floors. And it's becoming more difficult for smokers to gain employment in the workplace.

In April 1988 the Federal Aviation Administration passed regulations prohibiting smoking on domestic airline flights of less than two hours. Northwest Airlines went even further and banned smoking on *all* flights. New court cases have also turned against the tobacco industry.

Has the growth of Christianity caused elements of *reform* to take place in this country? It seems obvious; evidences of reform are everywhere. But what does reform have to do with the Church?

You are no doubt familiar with the "three R's of education." Are you aware of the "three *theological* R's"? They are *Regeneration, Revival,* and *Reformation.*

Regeneration is the operation of the Holy Spirit upon the individual, applying the atonement--the blood of Christ--to the *individual* for personal salvation.

A person may be saved (regenerated) and receive the blessings of God, including going to Heaven, by accepting the Lord Jesus Christ as personal Savior. First, he must realize that he is a sinner (". . . for ALL have sinned, and come short of the glory of God"---Romans 3:23) and that he is condemned to die ("For the wages of sin is death"---Romans 6:23).

Then the person must realize that God loves him so much that God gave His only begotten son, Jesus Christ, as his substitute--that Jesus bore his sin and died in his place ("He hath made *him* (Jesus) to be *sin* for *us,* who knew no sin; that *we* might *be made* the *righteousness* of God in *him*"--Corinthians 5:21). The person must realize that Christ was buried and was raised for his justification. Then he must call on the Lord for salvation ("For *whosoever* [that includes everyone] shall call upon the name of the Lord, *shall be saved*--Romans 10:13).

Regeneration (being born again) occurs when God's salvation is claimed by faith, according to His Word. The Philippian jailer asked Paul and Silas, "What must I do to be saved?"

Paul and Silas replied, "Believe on the Lord Jesus Christ, and Thou shalt be saved, and thy house." (Acts 16:31) This same regeneration occurs today when one calls upon the Lord, in faith, believing.

Revival is the operation of the Holy Spirit upon the *Church*. You cannot revive something that does not already have life. Revival brings the Church back to its essentials, with a fervent love for God and a desire to walk with Him in holiness.

Reformation is the effect of regeneration and revival on culture. You cannot *see* regeneration or revival (the work of the Holy Spirit); but you can see the *effects* as God's Word influences and reshapes the culture--that is *reform*.

The events, trends, and activities of people and organizations (some of which were listed earlier in this book) that occurred in the late 60's and 70's are *effects* of awakening.

What is the primary cause of this awakening? Where is

the evidence that God is intervening?

In the 1950's missionaries in Lebanon sent a young emigrant to America to attend Bible school. The young man, Sam Moore, sold Bibles to pay his way through Columbia Bible College. He was so successful at selling Bibles that in the 1960's he established his own company, Royal Publishers. In 1969 his company bought a bankrupt New York publishing house, Thomas Nelson. In 1970 Sam Moore's company began to print and market Bibles. From 1970 through the mid-80's, Sam Moore had published and marketed over 100 million Bibles.

Before World War II, the Bible had been the world's best seller. After the war, the *Communist Manifesto* and *Sayings of Chairman Mao* sold best around the world. By 1970 the "sex manual" boom displaced both the Bible and Communist literature on the world's best-seller lists.

However, by 1986, there was solid evidence that the Bible had once again regained the top spot. This is important. No reform effort or movement can succeed without God's influence through His Word.

In the September 2, 1985, edition of *TIME*, the cover article reported on "Thunder on the Right: the Growth of Fundamentalism." The magazine cover pictured Jerry Falwell.

On page 49 the magazine stated, "Fundamentalist legions seek to remake church and society." Elsewhere in the same article *TIME* wrote:

> From tiny rural chapels, where true believers seated on rickety folding chairs profess 'born again' faith, to handsome, stately churches like Falwell's, with memberships the size of a small town, Protestant Fundamentalism has been a powerful, confident, and important force. . . .

Also in this same article:

> Doctrinaire Protestantism is bursting beyond church walls into the wider society. Not since the 1920s have political Fundamentalists been so well financed, visible, organized, and effective.

SEPTEMBER 2, 1985 $1.95

TIME

Thunder on the Right
The Growth of Fundamentalism

The Reverend
Jerry Falwell

DUSTUP IN MOSCOW
Sparring over
Spies and
ASATS

(Remember, this is *TIME* magazine, not a Christian or conservative publication.)

TIME also wrote in the September 2, 1985 issue:

The Fundamentalists have moved into the center of America's culture stage . . . (page 49).

The years since World War II have brought a boom among both Evangelicals and Fundamentalists in youth ministries, foreign missions, day schools, publishing and broadcasting . . . (page 50).

Major denominations that take a more flexible approach to the interpretation of Scripture have suffered a net decline of 4.6 million members since 1965. In the same years the Southern Baptists alone increased by 3.4 million . . . (page 52).

Tim LaHaye's wife, Beverly, operates *Concerned Women for America* . . . . Begun in 1979, Concerned Women now boasts 500,000 members, more than the combined following of the National Organization of Women, the National Women's Political Caucus, and the League of Women Voters . . . (page 57).

The *TIME* article also observes, "The Movement is thin on culture awareness, scholarship and intellectual staying power" (page 57). For the most part, *TIME* is right in its observations. Many Christians are oblivious to what is going on; their convictions "burn out" sooner or later, or they take their Biblical convictions "for granted."

It is the Church's age-old battle against humanism. We are educated by humanists (in their institutions), so confusion is inevitable. If Christians are judged for "scholarship and intellectual staying power," should it be the humanists who set the standards?

Well, even by their standards, something significant is taking place. A *Reader's Digest*/Gallup Survey (1986) reports that:

> 95 percent of Americans believe in God.
> 87 percent pray.
> 70 percent have answers to prayer.
> 70 percent believe in the deity of Christ.

Another survey (by Tim LaHaye) says 62 percent of Americans believe that Jesus Christ is one day coming back.

While these statistics do not give precise figures on exact numbers of Christians and their faith, they do accurately reflect the *trends*.

A similar poll in 1954 had shown that church attendance and belief had "peaked" and begun to decline. The 1986 poll evidences a drastic reversal of that statistic and affirms that "belief" is up considerably.

There *are exact figures* to reflect the trends--the number of churches and Sunday schools have increased significantly and para-church works have also had an explosion of growth. The trends have spilled over into American society and culture and are having an effect:

--American college campuses are shifting back to the right.

--Wall Street is going through a period of soul-searching, with a renewed emphasis on ethics over greed.

--*Seven-Eleven, Eckerds*, and other retailers responded to Christian activism and removed pornography from their stores.

--*Playboy* closed its *Playboy Clubs* in Chicago, New York, and San Francisco, etc.

--*Wal-Mart* removed offensive "porn rock" records from its stores, and Congress held hearings on X-rated rock to consider a code or rating system for offensive records and tapes.

--*Grandy's* fast-food chain prints Scripture on its promotional coupons.

--The *U.S. Army* announced a new non-smoking regulation, banning smoking in ranks and vehicles, and nearly everywhere else on a base.

--The *U.S. Marine Corps* told Nathan Johnson, a new recruit in 1986, that things are now different at boot camp. The recruiting sergeant said there would be "no cussin', no pornography, no tobacco, no alcohol . . . and you *will* attend chapel."

Yet, even all these examples of Christianity having an effect on culture do not provide us with the *greatest* evidence that God is intervening. The greatest evidence is seen as God begins to *deal with sin*. In history God openly attacked idolatry; this is occurring TODAY in the most dramatic happening of the last two millenniums.

5

THE RESTORATION OF THE FAMILY

When society becomes decadent, in any age, one dominant sin usually becomes popular. It then surfaces as some form of "social *idolatry*."

Since the 1950's and 1960's, a sexual promiscuity has been increasingly practiced by the consensus (majority). In the 60's and 70's this consensus gave popular recognition of this sinful expression, and they named it the "Sexual Revolution." The Sexual Revolution was a form of social idolatry that flew in the face of God's ways. God's commandments were intended to develop and value the *family*.

The Sexual Revolution idolatry was a violation of the family structure and morals and was characterized by:

--Pornography.
--Easy divorce and child abandonment.
--Abortion.
--Incest and child abuse.
--Homosexuality and "gay rights."
--Sexual promiscuity in the guise of "free love."

--Anti-human values and sensuality in TV programming, music, movies, and other popular entertainment .
--Violence.
--Anti-Christian media and organizations.

In the guise of granting "rights" (to gays, feminists, pro-choice, and Planned Parenthood advocates, and so forth), the idolatry was given pseudo credibility and legitimacy. In the name of "freedom," "understanding," "consciousness raising," or "rights," these individuals and organizations (with common purposes) attempted to tear down the very fiber of American culture and the first institution that God ordained: *the family*.

However, God always deals with the sin of idolatry. Many times in Scripture God dealt with the sin of idolatry through a *plague*.

In recent times some people scoffed at the idea of a plague coming as some sort of divine retribution or means of dealing with sin. But no more. Even the cynical popular press is talking about the new plague of our generation: AIDS.

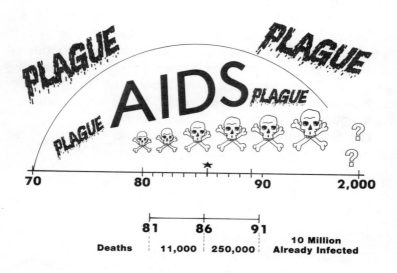

AIDS is not just the plague of our generation or lifetime. Dr. Alvin Kline of New York University calls AIDS the "plague of the millennium." Dr. Restak, a Washington, D.C., neurologist, agrees. She says AIDS can "wield a devastation such as has not been encountered on this planet in hundreds of years."

Also alarming is the fact that other sexually transmitted diseases are also multiplying in prairie-fire fashion. *Syphilis* was up 32 percent in 1987 in the U.S. *U.S. News and World Report* (March 21, 1988) tells of another startling trend: people may be simultaneously spreading both AIDS and virulent new forms of syphilis.

Another *15 million* Americans have incurable *herpes*. *Chlamydia* is exploding, along with gonorrhea. Doctors say, "Bacteria that cause *gonorrhea* are quickly developing resistance to another antibiotic and the world may be running out of drugs to cure this common venereal disease" (according to the *Dallas Morning News* (July 30, 1987). The article also stated, "We are beginning to run out of drugs . . . . The incidence of antibiotic-resistant gonorrhea has increased 30 times since 1980."

If matters were not already bad enough *NEWSWEEK* (January 4, 1988) reports that another AIDS virus has appeared on the scene. According to *U.S. News and World Report* (April 6, 1987), Dr. Jonathan Mann (director of the World Health Organization's AIDS program) stated, "There is a global epidemic of AIDS that leaves no country untouched." The article reports some 44,652 cases of AIDS from 99 countries, and W.H.O. estimates that *ten million* people are already infected. The April 14, 1988, issue of the same magazine stated that the reported number of AIDS cases has increased to 56,000--with some 31,000 deaths reported.

From 1981 to 1986, only 11,000 AIDS-related deaths were reported. Authorities now think that as many as a quarter million new AIDS cases will be reported during the five year period between 1987 and 1991.

In January 1988 health officials from 150 countries met in London and reported the global total of AIDS cases was already 75,000 *reported* cases. Officials think that the actual total may be *twice* that and will reach one million by 1991, according to *U.S. News* (February 8, 1988). The number of those contracting the "full-bloom" AIDS disease *doubles* every year.

Regarding AIDS, the *Journal of the A.M.A.* states, "The Human Immunodeficiency Virus is one of the *most* virulent infectious agents ever encountered. It kills up to one-half of the people infected. There is no safe or effective treatment, no vaccine . . . it invades the victim's cells, passes genetic material on to it, then the victim's body does the rest. The immunity system is rendered ineffective; it attacks the brain and the central nervous system, mutates rapidly and makes body defenses default."

Surgeon General Everett Koop has said that by 1990, sixty-four million Americans *could* be infected and ultimately one in four could die. The World Health Organization estimates that *100 million* could die before the AIDS plague subsides. That number is more than the combined population of Great Britain and France. That is probably more people than have died *in all the wars of history!*

The genetic mutations of the AIDS virus also abound; as a disease AIDS is evolving five times faster than normal. It is the most sinister disease in the history of medical science.

It is almost as if AIDS were the embodiment of evil, exposing its evil source and resources--primarily to the guilty of the *"Sex Revolution."*

AIDS is truly the plague of the millennium; and it simply illustrates the great Biblical principle:

"The wages of sin is death."

AIDS is truly a plague, a curse, on our sexual idolatry-- an idolatry that has even spread into the Church.

People ask how a loving God could permit such widespread horror. Even innocent babies and children contract AIDS and suffer. People express that it may be understandable and appropriate justice for the guilty to acquire AIDS, but why do the *innocent* suffer if the AIDS plague is

God's judgment for sex sin?

The young and the innocent have always suffered whenever the generation who is responsible commits sin. When a drunk drives his pick-up the wrong way on an expressway and hits a bus filled with church youth and kills 27-- or when another drunk runs a light and smashes another car, innocent people are often maimed and killed. To say God is responsible for AIDS is like saying the U.S. Department of Transportation is responsible for the 50,000 highway deaths every year.

No! The government writes the law, but the drivers break the rules. The violations are the cause of the suffering, not the lawgiver. In war the young and innocent also suffer. Man's sin always causes human suffering.

Will medical science find a cure for AIDS? That's the current subject of millions of dollars in research.

The fact of the matter is, we already have a cure. It is found in the pages of the Bible. AIDS is not a medical, social, or mechanical problem.

AIDS IS A *MORAL* PROBLEM.

In Kampola, Uganda, (where AIDS is widespread) Dr. Rick Goodgame, a missionary doctor, has received a favorable response from the Ugandan government to his unique program to counter AIDS. Dr. Goodgame believes that *Biblical teaching* on marriage and morality will help stem the spread of AIDS. His program has the approval of Uganda's Committee for AIDS Prevention. AIDS has already infected four million Africans, according to W.H.O. statistics.

Our thesis is that God began to intervene in modern events in and around 1970. But the AIDS plague was not manifest until 1981. Did God make a mistake? Did we misread the signs as to *when God began to intervene?* No, because the fact is AIDS has an incubation period of perhaps ten years or more. AIDS was simply *discovered* in 1981. This plague is the greatest evidence that God is intervening, for it is a work of righteousness that *only God could perform.*

The sexual idolaters experienced judgment on sins they

had committed earlier; the judgment was there even before AIDS was discovered. God is right on time.

The second area where God is at work in dealing with sin is in the Church. The events of the past few years show that more than a few evangelical and fundamentalist leaders have been caught up in the sexual idolatry of the world. Some were more widely publicized by the media than others, but they all reflect the reality of the problem:

> --One of the leaders of a great ministry in America was brought down after he was discovered using pornographic films at the ministry headquarters and being sexually involved with several staff women.
>
> --The son of a famous preacher, himself a young pastor with a great Midwestern church, had sexual affairs concurrently with three women from his congregation. He even had intimate relations in church offices during the Sunday school hour with one of the women (a deacon's wife) and then went out to preach. He was later caught, and his career and family ruined.
>
> --The leader of a nationwide TV ministry was nearly destroyed when the public learned of his sexual sin with a church secretary.
>
> --Less than a year later, another great TV preacher was humbled when he was discovered with a prostitute.
>
> --The head of one of the most effective evangelical ministries and inspiring Christian authors resigned after his adulterous affair was revealed.
>
> --A Christian musician for a large national radio ministry was fired when it was learned that he was a practicing homosexual.

These cases are just a few, a small fraction, of the cases made public. At least 23 prominent leaders have fallen in the last 24 months. Imagine how many other pastors, Christian leaders, and ministry role models have been involved in sexual sins which were *not* made public. Imagine, too, the multiplied numbers of *lay* Christians whose lives, careers, and marriages have been wrecked because they also practiced sexual idolatry.

Years ago, it was rare to hear about a pastor who ran off with a member of the church staff. Today nearly every town has a case study of just such a situation. Not just church members, but church leaders "buying into" the sexual revolution. The formula is universal:

$$\frac{\text{RATIONAL}}{\text{HUMANISM}} + \text{Affluence} + \frac{\text{Sexual}}{\text{Revolution}} = \text{LAODICEANISM}$$

After an evangelist had spoken on this theme, a youth pastor's wife came forward in the meeting in tears. She wept as she told the pastor in charge about the pornographic magazines to which her husband was addicted. "He keeps them beside our bed and uses them in place of natural feelings of love one for another," she cried. She felt used and abused by her husband's sexual idolatry.

The world, through the sensation-hungry media, revels in the sins of the Church. But we must point out that Jesus said it would be "shouted from the housetops"--not because God chooses to embarrass the church, but this is a human form of cleansing. God desires correction and restoration. He will not permit the Church to continue in sin, and He will eventually deal with the world and its sin.

Ephesians 5:1-7 teaches that believers should not pattern their behavior after the world. The Apostle Paul tells us to walk in love and to be imitators of God. We are told to avoid sexual sin (verse 3), and filthiness and unclean conversation (verse 4).

God warns about the sin of sexual idolatry (verse 5)--and of God's wrath which will come (verse 6). He concludes, "Be not ye therefore partakers with them."

God will purge and discipline His Church as well as the world. God has a "woodshed" and recently a number of evangelical and fundamentalist leaders have been in for an appointment. God uses this "woodshed experience" not for *"punishment,"* but for *"correction."* Some submit to the correction, accountability, cleansing, and healing. Within a year or two they are restored once again to their ministry. But others chafe and resist the correction. They spend a longer time in the "woodshed." Some are never restored.

God's woodshed may reap diseases of peril or shame and embarrassment in this unusual Laodicean era, but His hand has been revealed. God Himself has intervened! What is He doing? The PLAGUE and the WOODSHED are God's ways of bringing about the

RESTORATION OF THE FAMILY

AND THE

CLEANSING OF THE CHURCH.

6

THE THIRD GREAT AWAKENING

The first great period of God's intervention during modern times was at the coming of the Pilgrims and Puritans to America. They came to the New World to set up communities structured according to their religious beliefs and convictions, whereby they could walk with God.

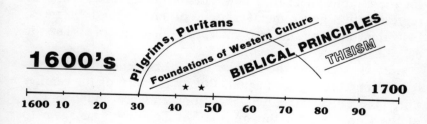

Their plan was successful and a number of Godly communities were established, governed by Christian principles and laws based on Biblical, *Theistic* beliefs.

But soon, the migration to the new territory of unbelievers from Europe and other parts of the world began to dilute this Theistic culture. By the early 1700,s (about a century after the first pilgrim settlements) the ministers reported that most of their church members had not been born again. By the third generation (grandchildren of the original settlers), the church was Christian in name only.

During the 1720's and 1730's, men of God appeared somewhat spontaneously on the scene. Johann Freylinghausen, a German pietist clergyman; the great preacher Jonathan Edwards; preacher-evangelist George Whitefield; and the brothers John and Charles Wesley preached repentance, salvation, and holiness. What followed, historians call *"The Great Awakening."*

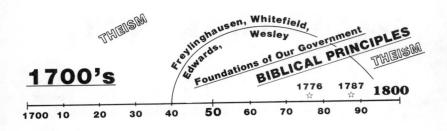

The Great Awakening prepared the American colonies for the establishment of a new "nation under God," with its representative government, system of checks and balances, individual liberty, and free enterprise--all fruits of a Theistic culture.

By the peak of the Awakening, 20 percent of New England claimed to be born again. But by the turn of the century (after the establishment of U.S. independence and adoption of the Constitution), the spiritual awakening began again to decline.

The Industrial Revolution had begun and was having a major impact on immigration. This time great masses flooded into the young, free country where opportunity abounded.

As America's riches and its citizens' material wealth increased, the nation grew cold in its spiritual commitment.

Thus blinded, the country grew callous and permitted slavery as a means to prosper America's economy. But slavery also divided the country. President Abraham Lincoln called on the nation to fast, pray, and seek after God. Nevertheless, a great civil war shook America.

Just a few years earlier, however, a young Ohio lawyer began an inquiry into Christianity and the Bible. As a result, Charles Finney was converted and became an itinerant preacher. In 1855 he began to go into factories and mill towns to preach the Gospel.

Factory owners even shut down the factories while workers gathered to hear Finney preach from God's Word. Evangelist D. L. Moody and his ministry fueled the revival. By the 1870's the revival had spread. At its peak some 50,000 to 60,000 conversions were reported happening in America every week.

Moody also went overseas and sparked revivals in Great Britain. He is said to have brought England and America back together--and back to God.

Once again an *Awakening* was building.

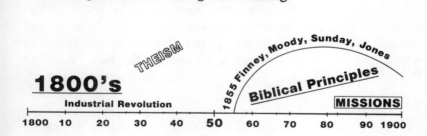

At the peak of this second "Great Awakening," 20 percent of all Americans claimed to be "born again."

By the end of the nineteenth century, another great spiritual movement began to occur, born out of the Second Great Awakening. It was the great thrust in world missions.

Between 1885 and 1900, doors were opened for the Gospel to be preached in nearly every nation. This movement gave the greatest impetus to the Great Commission since its introduction. The last 15 years of the nineteenth century put the *greatest number of people in the history of the Church* into a pulpit ministry and onto the mission field.

This period is called by historians "The Second Great Awakening" and introduced the period to follow, known as the "evangelistic era."

This spiritual movement continued into the twentieth century through the work of Billy Sunday, Bob Jones, Sam Morris, and others; but its influence was dampened by World War I, the revolution in Russia, and the so-called "flapper era." Morals began to decline and humanism entered the academic world. The economy was inflated, and by October 1929 the economy had utterly collapsed. By the 1930's dramatic changes began to occur not only in economics, but also in government, education, and even religion.

Following World War II, by judicial review, the Bible was removed from government schools. By 1954 church attendance had peaked and started to decline as Americans turned toward "the good life." Humanist writers and leaders had boasted that they would rewrite the textbooks and bring about cultural changes.

By the 1960's American campuses bore the fruits of this change. Major university campuses erupted in violence and chaos. Activist Jerry Rubin paced this trend of rebellion which spread from Columbia University in New York to Berkeley in California. Even small local institutions were affected.

Culture, by 1968, had become degenerate. The late Christian theologian-philosopher Dr. Francis Schaeffer remarked, "It drags the ground."

Christians perceived 1968 as the absolute bottom of their culture and it drove them to desperation. (It was this background period that *TIME* and *NEWSWEEK* wrote about in 1988 in separate retrospective cover stories about 1968.)

The morality of our culture (described in Chapter Two) was so obviously corrupt by the late 60's that Christians in many differing denominations began to pray.

Once again--

GOD INTERVENED.

The Word of God, working in and through believers, spontaneously began to influence society and have an impact. Contemporary movements, similar in principle to those of the 1700's and 1800's, began to surface. New programs, styles, approaches, ideas, and labels began to emerge and have an impact on such cultural institutions as education, family life, and the church.

In 1976 the U.S. Government Office of Statistics reported that 34 percent of Americans claimed to be "born again." Christians--for the first time in this century--had a major influence on the 1976 election.

Did the statistics mean that 34 percent of all Americans were genuinely converted and living a holy Christian life-style? Probably not. The statistics simply meant that 34 percent claimed to be born again.

All we can honestly conclude is that more people claimed to be born again (in 1976) than at any previous time in U.S. history. Yet, by 1984, the percentage had risen even higher, to 40 percent--which means 40 percent of a 240-million population (96 million) claim to be born again.

Are these Christians having an influence and impact on culture?

Consider that this is an age of "Laodiceanism":

$$\frac{\text{RATIONAL}}{\text{HUMANISM}} + \text{Affluence} + \frac{\text{Sexual}}{\text{Revolution}} = \text{LAODICEANISM}$$

American Christians --both the remnant living relatively separated and holy lives and the "Laodiceans" who have "bought into" a compromised culture--represent the "luke-warm" church as described in Revelation 3:14-19:

> And unto the angel of the church of the Laodiceans write; These things saith the Amen, the faithful and true witness, the beginning of the creation of God; I know thy works, that thou art neither cold nor hot: I would thou wert cold or hot. So then because thou art lukewarm, and neither cold nor hot, I will spue

thee out of my mouth. Because thou sayest, I am rich, and increased with goods, and have need of nothing; and knowest not that thou art wretched, and miserable, and poor, and blind, and naked: I counsel thee to buy of me gold tried in the fire, that thou mayest be rich; and white raiment, that thou mayest be clothed, and that the shame of thy nakedness do not appear; and anoint thine eyes with eyesalve, that thou mayest see. As many as I love, I rebuke and chasten: be zealous therefore, and repent.

This lukewarm "Laodicean" church is living in the last definable period of the Church Age (a time when man and the Church are at their worst) and at the time of God's final intervention--a time which immediately precedes the Apocalypse. Because the Church, in Western culture, is affluent and carnal does not diminish the fact that it is still the Church. The Corinthian church which Paul addressed was "carnal" and "walked as babes," but it was still the Church. The Church--caught up in Western culture, with its affluence, rational humanism, and "sex revolution"--is now under the corrective hand of God. It is STILL THE CHURCH--and this "Laodicean Church" is the Church for which Christ will return.

The effects of God's intervention:

> Regeneration . . .
> Revival . . . and
> Reformation.

Again, these are the "three theological R's" referred to earlier. By way of reminder, *regeneration* results in new birth in *individuals; revival* brings new life to the *Church*; and *reform* affects *culture*.

Man is arrogant, ignorant, and hostile to God, or may even reject God. But God does His work regardless of the character of the culture, its influence on the Church, or the Church's perceived quality of spirituality. In other words,

God often works *in spite* of His people, not *because* of them.

In 1970 the Holy Spirit intervened in a period of what this writer refers to as the

THIRD GREAT AWAKENING.

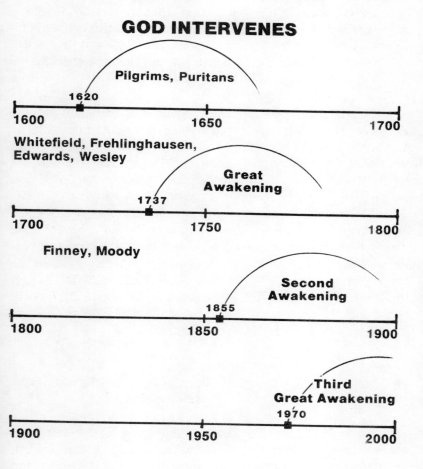

GOD INTERVENES

Pilgrims, Puritans

1620

1600   1650   1700

Whitefield, Frehlinghausen, Edwards, Wesley

Great Awakening

1737

1700   1750   1800

Finney, Moody

Second Awakening

1855

1800   1850   1900

Third Great Awakening

1970

1900   1950   2000

7

WHEN WILL JESUS CHRIST RETURN?

The period from 1970 to 2000 will be the greatest period of evangelism, missions, church growth, Christian school development, preaching, teaching, and witnessing in the entire history of the world.

The material documented in the first few chapters of this book was presented in 1986 to over 15,000 Christian educators in the *Accelerated Christian Education* fall conventions. The material was given to audiences in every state and was entitled "God Is Intervening."

In December of that same year, my family and I went to the mountains of Colorado for the holidays and a brief vacation. During this period I spent time in research and reflection to answer these questions:

1. How will the Third Great Awakening affect the rest of the world?

2. What effect will the Third Great Awakening have on the twenty-first century?

After a week of research, I began to ask, "Will there *even be* a twenty-first century?"

In studying the two questions with which I originally began, I concentrated on Mark 16:15 and Matthew 28:19-20, referred to in Biblical chronology as "The Great Commission."

Next, the prophetic teachings of Matthew 24 (called the "Olivet Discourse") became my focus of study. I began to see the Third Great Awakening in a "Great Commission" eschatological context.

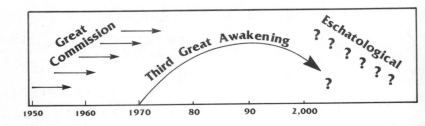

It was amazing to see how these Scriptures related to contemporary events, especially those events referred to in the earlier chapters of this book. From 1968 until the present, the application was especially startling.

There is an abundance of evidence that God is intervening, not just in the United States but on a global scale--with overwhelming evidence of His intervention in Indonesia, China, India, Southeast Asia, the South Pacific, South and Central America, Africa, and even Israel, as well as other nations.

This intervention was brought home to me during two visits I made to China--one in 1982 and another in 1986. It was confirmed even more in 1987 when I made repeat visits to Great Britain, Europe, South Africa, and the South Pacific. Some parts of the world were missing God's hand of blessing, and others were seeing miraculous evidence of His presence and intervening power.

Personal contacts and background knowledge gained from previous trips abroad added to this understanding, with an awareness of what was also happening in Central and South America. God was intervening in many Latin countries, a fact confirmed during my December 1987 visit to the Palace of Santa Domingo in the Dominican Republic.

The Great Commission (Mark 16:15) commands believers to ". . . Go ye into *all* the world, and *preach* the gospel to every creature."

"All the world" was the command given 1950 years ago, at a time when men did not have any of the efficient, modern means to do so. In A.D. 33 men did not have 747 jumbo jets to circle the world in a day or so. They had no ocean liners, trains, autos, bicycles--or even roller skates. Consider the past and present implications of this command which Jesus gave to a handful of simple and uneducated men.

"Preach . . . to every creature." When this command was first given it must have seemed unreasonable. Yet, the early disciples had only a vague concept of the size and shape of the earth. They had never seen an atlas or globe; there were no aerial photos or satellite maps. The disciples had no radios, films, televisions, tape cassette or record players--or even a printing press. They had not even a vague perception of the scope of that commission, much less the tools it would have taken to complete the task.

Therefore, we must conclude that not only was God, in the Lord Jesus, giving this comprehensive commission to just this handful of disciples--He was also giving the instructions to all believers of the two millenniums that have transpired since the commission was given.

Matthew 28:19,20 is another account of the Great Commission: *"Go* ye therefore, and *teach* all nations, *baptizing* them in the name of the Father, and of the Son, and of the Holy Ghost: *teaching* them to observe all things whatsoever I have commanded you: and, lo, I am with you alway, even unto the *end* of the *world*. Amen."

"Teach . . .baptizing them." The substance of the message was Jesus Himself. The teaching centered in Him, and the baptizing was to illustrate the life committed to Him and to confirm the person's loyalty to Him.

". . . *Unto the end of the world*." This did not mean the

end of everything, but rather the end of an age; that is, the end of the significance for and objectives of the preaching, teaching, and baptizing.

This Great Commission became the "marching orders" for the Church and is directly related to a comprehensive message that Jesus had taught His disciples approximately 15 days earlier on the Mount of Olives. Jesus had presented the *Olivet Discourse* just before His triumphal entry into Jerusalem, the trial and Crucifixion that followed, the Resurrection, and the events surrounding the giving of the Great Commission.

The Olivet Discourse provided clear-cut descriptions and questions and answers about "the end of the world," as well as Jesus' definitive designation: *"then shall the end come."*

The discussions of Matthew 24 and 25 deal unmistakably with the "end of the age." The distinctive features of this "end-time" period are listed in the context of Jesus' Olivet Discourse. They clearly and significantly characterize the exact period in which we are now living.

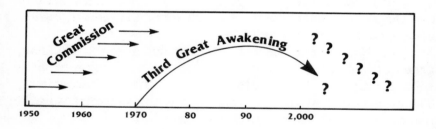

When read in context with Matthew 23, the Olivet Discourse (Matthew 24) is more easily understood. In Chapter 23 Jesus wept over Jerusalem--which was the *past world capital* (under David and Solomon) and will be the *future world capital* (under Christ Himself as "King of Kings and Lord of Lords").

Verse 38, ". . . your house is left unto you desolate," is interesting. The "house" could be the nation or people of which God was the *theocratic* head and the political and religious leader, with "desolate" meaning the presence and power of God would be removed.

Matthew 24, verses 1 and 2, tell of the coming fulfillment of that prophecy. Jesus describes the impending destruction of Jerusalem in A.D. 70.

He then led the disciples through the Eastern Gate, down through the valley, and up to the Mount of Olives. Jesus sat down, overlooking the Temple which was clearly visible a mile or so to the West. His disciples came to Him with questions.

Three specific questions are recorded and, no doubt, are most significant for consideration since they provide for the substance and teaching that follows in the rest of Matthew 24 and 25:

1. "When shall these things be?"
2. "What shall be the sign of thy coming . . .?
3. ". . . and of the end of the world?"

Matthew 24:3

The answers which Jesus gave bridged the time from the then present to an unknown "end-time" period heretofore unrecognizable.

"When shall these things be?" refers, no doubt, to the prophecy in verse two concerning Jerusalem's destruction, which actually took place about 40 years after the discourse. The prophecy was quite literal: "There shall not be left here one stone upon another." And it happened just that way.

When the Temple was destroyed and burned to the ground, the gold decorations melted and ran between the cracks of the floor and walls. The Romans actually dug through the rubble and pried up even the foundation stones, looking for gold in the debris, thus fulfilling Jesus' prophecy- -not "one stone upon another."

"What shall be the sign of thy coming, and the end of the world?" Christ's (Second) Coming and the end of this world are two critical matters phrased in a complex answer. Matthew 24:4-14 answers both questions. It describes the character of the "end-time" period and gives clues to events

that will be associated with the Lord's return.

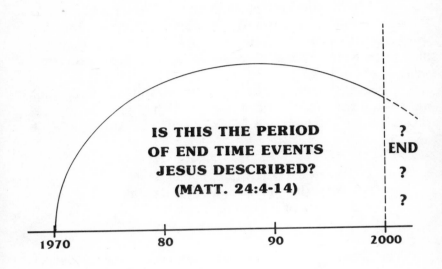

IS THIS THE PERIOD
OF END TIME EVENTS
JESUS DESCRIBED?
(MATT. 24:4-14)

?
END
?
?

1970   80   90   2000

These 11 verses are the most significant verses on eschatology related to this period in the Bible. *Eschatology* is traditionally defined as the doctrine of the "last days" or "end-time events." No other passage of Scripture seems to shed as much light on end-time events as Matthew 24:4-14.

"*Many shall come in my name, saying, I am Christ; and shall deceive many*" (verse 5). This has occurred in the past, but in the last third of this century, the impostors are multiplying. With the capabilities of mass media, the announcements have far more *significance* than at any previous time in history.

This full page ad appeared in newspapers across America.

"*Ye shall hear of wars and rumours of wars*" (verse 6).
There have always been such conflicts between tribes and nations. This prediction could apply to any age except for the
significance of the *context*. The scale of "wars and rumours
of wars" has grown in unbelievable proportions during this
century. World War I brought all the "civilized" nations of
the earth into international war. The Second World War,
which occurred in the middle of this century, followed this
same pattern and left the world divided between East and
West. Entire populations were exterminated by Hitler, Stalin,
Mao Tse Tung, Idi Amin, and Pol Pot, as "nations" and
"kingdoms" fought.

An exploding population and technology have brought
people closer together geographically, but the conflict between families, tribes, and small and great nations continues

and intensifies. Men and entire countries are divided over land, language, culture, tradition, politics, religion--and even leadership personalities. Each nuclear disarmament summit points to the fact of world division: "kingdom against kingdom."

Today over 40 nations are at war. Over 100 nations are involved in some kind of local violence or internal civil war.

"There shall be famines . . ." (verse 7). The huge number of people living in today's world multiplies the odds in favor of a famine and increases the significance and scope of such an occurrence. In recent years, major famines have killed *millions of people* in Bangladesh, India, Ethiopia (another two million are expected to die during 1988 and 1989 in Ethiopia), and several other countries in Africa and Asia. These famines, with the resulting statistics of deaths and dying, are undoubtedly the most significant in all history and effectively characterize Jesus' words in Matthew 24:7.

Not only that, recent famines have become even more critical. Wars and droughts have plagued people in many nations where Communists have used these natural disasters to their own advantage, sometimes starving people into submission or simply allowing their extinction as a result of the famines.

" . . . And pestilence" (verse 7). Scientists tell us that increasing numbers of insects and bacteria have become immune to DDT or anti-bacterial drugs. Various kinds of chemical insecticides have passed on and off the scene to which succeeding generations of insects have built an immunity. Great numbers of insects like the Mediterranean fruit fly have begun to plague farms in unusual ways. These new and more virulent species of insects have grown in a scope of increasing scale and complexity.

The side effects of man's efforts to control insects have had equally disastrous results. DDT in the food chain of the environment has imperiled vast numbers of birds, the "natural" control for insect populations. Genetic experiments have also let matters get out of control. So-called "killer bees" were once a science fiction fantasy; now they are real.

New and exotic bacteria and viruses are multiplying throughout the world; many kinds are building up an immunity to drugs and other efforts designed to control them. Hong Kong flu, legionnaire's disease, and certain allergies exist today that were apparently unheard of in earlier years.

AIDS and the newer virulent strains of venereal diseases (syphilis, herpes, gonorrhea, chlamydia), which, according to health authorities, already exist in epidemic proportions worldwide, are among the most sinister and devastating forms of pestilence in our contemporary world. Certainly the significance, scope, and frequency of pestilence is far greater now than in Jesus' day, or in any era since.

" . . . *And earthquakes in divers places*" (verse 7). Since 1970 earthquakes have increased dramatically in number, frequency, and severity. Earthquakes have occurred during the past few years not only in the "earthquake zones"--Japan, Iran, Alaska, China, and the west coasts of North and South America--but also in places least expected, such as the U.S. Midwest.

On July 10, 1987, Chicago's eight million people experienced earth tremors for the first time in modern history. The shock measured 3.5 on the Richter scale and was felt as far to the east as Ohio and Pennsylvania and to the south as Kentucky and Missouri. Two days later, Knoxville, Tennessee, felt another 3.5 earthquake. No one was hurt in these tremors, and there were only a few deaths in the Southern California earthquakes that occurred later that fall.

However, just about a year earlier (on September 19-21, 1986) Mexico City experienced a most terrible earthquake. Over 4200 died in a devastating 8.1 super quake. Just ten years earlier, an earthquake in Tangshan, China, killed 242,000--nearly a *quarter of a million people!*

Volcanic eruptions are also related to earthquakes. In the northwestern United States, Mt. St. Helens exploded on May 18, 1980. Volcanic ash and lava destroyed trees, grasslands, and crops for many miles. The volcanic ash and smoke plume rose several miles into the air and blocked out the sun.

"El Nino" was a similar atmospheric cloud of volcanic debris which affected the weather of the southwestern United

States, Mexico, and several other Latin America countries. On November 13, 1985, a volcano erupted in Colombia, South America. Deadly mud slides roared down the mountainsides in Nevado del Ruiz, and 22,940 people were killed.

"All these are the beginning of sorrows" (verse 8). Jesus seems to indicate (verses 2-8) that these specific signs will signal to the alert believer that the end is fast approaching, and that matters will likely even get worse (verses 9-41).

Matthew 24 is not meant to be simply outlined or read casually. Very few of Jesus' teachings were meant to be understood by just a surface reading or a study accompanied by unbelief. Understanding comes from a heart of willing acceptance and a mind open to God's revelation--"He that hath ears to hear, let him hear."

Perhaps the best outline for the Olivet Discourse in Matthew 24 is *geographical:*

> I. General *Worldwide* Signs (verses 4-8)--
> "The beginning of sorrows"

> II. Mideast *Regional* Signs (verses 9-29)
> (See also Daniel 9:27; 11-3; 12:1.)

It appears that neither Daniel nor succeeding generations of prophets and teachers were to be able to understand Daniel's prophecies, *until the time of the end*. Daniel 12:4 indicates they would remain a mystery and be "shut up *until the time of the end*."

Now, as end-time prophecies are being fulfilled and the context of the *"end-time" is coming into clear focus for the believer, there is a far greater general knowledge of Biblical prophecy than ever before*. Prophetic events are obviously coming to pass.

Pressure on Israel is another "sign." Hostility has intensified during Israel's recent 40-year history. Israel has hardly known a time of peace since she was established as a nation in May 1948.

Increased Palestinian pressure (from all of the Arab world) as well as pressure from the United Nations, the world press, and other countries continues to intensify. It almost seems as if there is a world conspiracy against Israel's claim to its land and independence as a nation. The names of Israel's enemies have become household items in the West as the media has expounded on the "excesses, hostility, and terrorist activities" of Israel. The international "squeeze" is tightening, and the conditions of Biblical prophecy surrounding the "nation of nations" are coming into clear and sharp focus--leading up to the Battle of Armageddon itself.

III. Other Worldwide Signs (verses 14; 30-36)

All tribes and nations of the earth will experience a preaching of the Gospel before a *visible* coming of the Lord Jesus Christ. (Exactly when will Christ's visible return take place? Jesus simply tells us, ". . . of that day and hour knoweth no man" (verse 36).

IV. Signs for the *West* and *Other Parts of the World* (verses 37-41)

It would appear these verses refer to the Americas, Europe, Africa, and Asia. The people seem to be living natural and normal lives, unaffected by the chaos in the Middle East.

Jesus described what will happen when individuals are "taken." Theologians describe this event as the *rapture*, the event which will (for believers) be the climax of all history.

Although no one knows exactly the day and hour of Jesus' return, we do have the signs that Jesus Himself gave us so that we can *know* with a great degree of accuracy when His *coming* is near. This passage is the guide to our understanding of this coming event (verses 4-14) and of the "times of the *end*."

Jesus told us to *watch* (verse 42) as that day quickly approaches. He gave pre-apocalyptic symptoms that believers should be able to recognize, and said, "THEN SHALL THE END COME."

8

GLOBAL POPULATION IS OPENING TO THE GOSPEL

Although the four great periods of religious development in fairly recent times were tremendous spiritual events, they did not usher in the Second Coming of Jesus Christ or mark the "end times."

The Reformation of the 1500's gave to the world not only Luther's vision of salvation by grace through faith alone, but also his vision for "Christian schools." The Reformation in England produced the Scriptures in the language of the people when the King James Bible was introduced in 1611. On the crest of that same wave, the Pilgrims and Puritans traveled to the New World to set up Christian communities and establish "one nation under God" for all the world to see.

The Great Awakening that gave a new political system (the Declaration of Independence and the Constitution) provided the climate for free enterprise to flourish and an Industrial Revolution to take place. The Second Great Awakening gave modern Christianity a scope and outreach for its faith. Believers from America and Great Britain opened every continent to Christianity and the Gospel. The Industrial Revolution financed this world missions thrust.

The inventions, wealth, and progress of the twentieth century provided for the implementation of global travel and communications for the Third Great Awakening. The following chart indicates the significance of these advances.

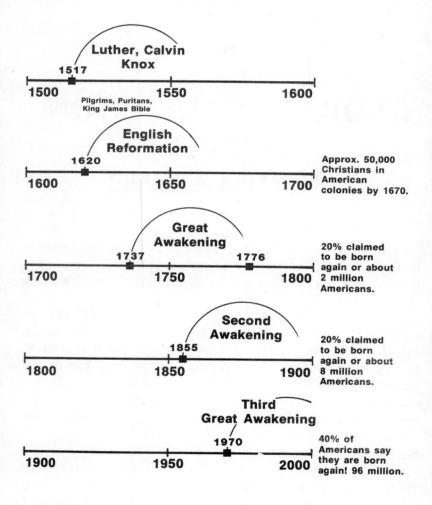

The actual number of *true* "born again" Christians would be impossible to determine. Because a certain number of people claim to be Christians or to have experienced the new birth does not verify that number as fact in Heaven. For our purposes, however, let us simply *compare* the number of persons making a confession as to the Christian faith. What is significant in this comparison is that there were *two million* professing Christians in the 1700's, as opposed to over *70 million* today.

In 1949 a young evangelist named Billy Graham held the first of many evangelistic "crusades." Hundreds, and then thousands, were saved at those events. However, the ratio of persons in the general population claiming to be born again did not change appreciably from that 20 percent factor. It was not until the 1970's that this ratio began to change. Today, according to pollster George Gallup Jr., some 96 million Americans--or 40 percent of the U.S. population--say they are born again.

Another *significant* factor can be seen in contemporary trends. If the statistics do not equal Heavenly facts, then the *trends* are living evidence of spiritual influence and change. Statistics are impressive, but trends are even more compelling.

	1978	1986	1987
American adults who have had religious training	17%	26%	
American teens who are engaged in Bible study	27%	41%	
American adults who share their faith (witness)	44%	53%	
Church membership		60%	65%
Church attendance		40%	45%

(These statistics may have up to a five percent rate of error. Twenty years ago, Sunday morning traffic was the lowest of the entire week and very few people were attending church. That has dramatically changed from the early 70's.)

Here is a startling fact from George Gallup, Jr: "More Americans attended church in 1986 in an *average week* than attended *all* professional baseball, basketball, and football games *combined* for an *entire year*."

Another poll (conducted in January 1987 by *U.S.A. Weekend Magazine*) gives the following facts:

> 94 percent of Americans have read some part of the Bible.
> 27 percent of Americans have read the *entire* Bible.
> 20 percent of Americans say they *read* the Bible *daily*.
> 60 percent of Americans say they talk to God (pray), rather than just saying prayers.
> 50 percent of homes with children say grace before meals.

In February 1988 I met George Gallup, Jr. in Washington, D.C., where we were both attending the *National Religious Broadcasters* convention. He told me how his father founded the Gallup Poll organization in the 1930's and how he had been involved since his youth with his father's work of gathering and interpreting statistics.

George Gallup, Jr. told me that he was confident that America was currently experiencing a great period of "awakening." The trends all reflect this greater involvement in and commitment to the matters of Christian faith and action.

Another aspect of this significance is what is happening in *missions*. Missions is a good test of spiritual commitment. People may attend church with little more than a casual interest in spiritual matters. But seldom do people pack their bags and leave home and family to move to a foreign country when they possess little more than a casual commitment to spiritual matters.

Actually, missionary activity on the part of Americans seems to have declined during the last generation. Following

World War II, thousands of young men and women volunteered to become overseas missionaries. Many saw the need while they were servicemen and after returning home responded to God's call upon their lives.

However, during the 1950's and 1960's, along with declining church membership, missions also declined. The fact is that by 1968 there were only about 35,000 American missionaries on the foreign fields, and one-third to one-half of these had gone out immediately after World War II and were approaching retirement age.

The significance of 1968 and its negative impact upon the world underscored the decline in missions. However, at the leading edge of the Third Great Awakening (beginning in 1970) this trend began to reverse itself. In the ten years between 1970 and 1980, there were some 54,000 American missionaries on foreign fields--more than a 50 percent increase. In addition to that, the entire *native* or *nationals* missionary movement exploded in overseas nations. Billy Graham's Lausanne and Amsterdam Conventions were catalysts, bringing thousands of native missionaries together for evangelism training. Others (like Bill Bright, John Haggai, and the late Bob Pierce) have also caught this missionary vision for helping nationals reach their own people for Christ.

Yet, this is not the most significant aspect of the missions explosion during the Third Great Awakening. New facts and trends point to events and activities that are so spectacular and dramatic that the Christian Church has not seen anything like it since her first days, as depicted in the book of Acts. I am referring to the outpouring of God's Spirit upon His Church everywhere in the world--especially in countries of the "Third World."

Developing nations that have received the Gospel in this century (since the Second Great Awakening) are becoming involved in missions. On my first trip to the Philippines, I preached in a small *barrio* church at Supang Bato. The church was very poor. Even though the people could hardly afford to turn on the lights and could not pay the pastor a salary, that small village church had a missionary they supported--a missionary to another country.

The same thing is happening in other Third World countries. Even in their poverty, Christians are setting up *mission agencies* and sending out *missionaries*. Note this amazing TREND:

Third World	*1972*	*1980*	*1986*
Agencies	200	368	1000 +
Missionaries	3400	13,000	32,000

These statistics do not take into consideration the missionary activity *within* the countries themselves. Tens of thousands of Christian workers, evangelists, and pastors are carrying on traditional missionary activity among their own people. In India alone, an estimated 50,000 native missionaries go from village to village preaching the Gospel.

The statistics in the table above are for missionaries *who are sent* to other countries. Missions experts predict that by A.D. 2000 churches in the Third World will have over 50,000 *foreign missionaries* on the field. Already, missionaries from Korea are reaching out to the Koreans living in the Houston area. Missionaries from Brazil are in Southern California ministering to their countrymen living in the great Los Angeles basin.

The substance of Truth, Ideals, Perfection, and Absolutes is on the RIGHT. The Left is the furthest extreme from that basic element. Evil in Scripture does not have substance; it is a departure *from* that substance or an absence of that good. Righteousness is an absolute expressing God's character, measuring the mark of deity. Sin is to "miss the mark." "Thou shalt not kill" is an absolute. Hegel said, "There are no absolutes." He was over on the Left.

```
Left                                    Right
Relative                                Absolute
No Values                               Ideals
Man                                     God
Humanism    ◄──── Philosophy ────►     Theism
```

ATHEISM◄THEOLOGY→BIBLICAL THEISM

The quality of a people's character determines their politics, and a people's real spiritual depth determines the quality of their character.

Alexander Hamilton said, "A people get the kind of government they deserve." The truth is, government is merely a reflection of the *character* of the people. Therefore, the greatest influence in bringing about a shift to the right is the increased influence of *righteousness* in the character of the people.

A shift toward democratic or righteous principles on the part of a nation or a leader may be the reflection of a spiritual awakening of some kind in the lives of the people of that country. ("Righteousness exalteth a nation.")

The United States became a great country and a leading nation in the world because of her great spiritual awakenings. These spiritual revivals powerfully affected both the people and the government. Currently, many developing Third World nations are experiencing their own "Great Awakening."

Righteousness is not always welcomed, as evidenced by problems in some Latin American and African countries. Certain political crises and "bloodletting" in some countries may be effects of Awakening. This spiritual activity does not promote violence, but violence is often incited when people who are not spiritual are inadvertently affected by rapid change. Those who are not spiritual may have ideas for their own kind of political changes. Violence, resistance, and military coups might even be reactions to or results of *spiritual* change, or by-products of political change.

The international pendulum is obviously swinging back to the right in a majority of countries, even in Communist and terrorist- or dictator-run countries. Eighty percent of the *total global* population are responding to some mysterious worldwide influence and are now open to the Gospel.

It may be that America, Great Britain, and Europe are going through a period of transition. There are evidences of Awakening in these nations, but the greatest and most significant events and activities are happening *elsehere*.

The Third Great Awakening has spread to nearly every nation on earth and is having a powerful influence and impact, unprecedented in the history of mankind. The Third Great Awakening is becoming a--

WORLD AWAKENING.

9

WORLD AWAKENING

Where would you look to find the largest Christian church in the world? London, New York, Chicago? Is it in Dallas, or Los Angeles?

Actually, the world's largest Christian church is not even in the Western Hemisphere. It is in Seoul, South Korea. (This fact may help give focus to the scope and influence of the Third Great Awakening and its effect all over the world.)

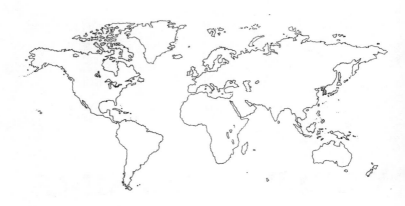

Korea

The effects of the world missions thrust of the Second Great Awakening did not reach Korea. In 1890 there was not a single Christian church in that country, and only a handful of believers were won to Christ during the next half-century.

In 1950 Korea was engaged in a civil war that brought other nations into the conflict. The Koreans experienced enormous terror, suffering, and hardship as they became pawns of world powers in history's first war fought for "limited political objectives." In 1953, the truce was signed dividing the country into North and South Korea at the 38th parallel (I was a young Marine aboard the U.S.S. General Black en route to serve in the U.N. forces at that time).

The war had a sobering effect on the Korean people: they were poor, wounded, and stripped of their dignity and pride. When American missionaries came to share God's love and redemption, the Korean people opened their hearts. They responded to the Gospel by the thousands.

By 1970 ten percent of the South Koreans were professing Christians; by 1980 that number doubled. By 1984 some 30 percent of the South Koreans professed Christ as Savior, and by 1986 this number increased to 33 percent, including 47 percent of the Army. Seoul had 6000 Christian churches by 1986, and *new churches* were being opened at the rate of *six per week.*

The *world's largest Methodist church,* with over 10,000 members, is located in Seoul. The *world's largest Presbyterian church* is also situated in Seoul; this church has over *50,000 members.* In 1986 Seoul also claimed the *world's largest Pentecostal church, with over a half-million members!* It was purported by 1988 to have reached 800,000 members.

When my son Daniel and I visited Seoul in 1982, we visited this Pentecostal church, eager to see if it was truly a Bible-believing church. First we stood outside and watched as what seemed to be a fleet of buses pulled up to multiple lines of people. The buses quickly discharged huge crowds coming to the worship service, and just as quickly gobbled up the waiting masses leaving the church. The scene was not unlike the shift change in front of a large factory.

Inside the church we were awed by the immenseness of the building and the crowd of worshipers. Over 13,000 people attended this service, which was identical to the 9 a.m. service and the 1 p.m., 3 p.m., and 5 p.m. services to follow. The church is now reported to be meeting in its new facility that seats over 35,000.

We sat in a section for foreign guests. The section was equipped with headphones labeled in different languages. We listened to the preaching in

English. The worship service included communion. We watched amazed as a battalion of deacons dispersed into the huge crowd. The deacons were carrying what would have been a *truckload* of silver communion service trays.

Why have one-third of South Koreans become Christians? There are probably many contributing factors. A recent survey found that most pastors spend at least an hour a day in prayer and 47 percent spend two or more hours daily in prayer.

Still, the media seems blind to this amazing phenomenon. The press reports political and economic changes, but does not perceive them as direct results of spiritual awakening.

South Korea's people are helping the nation become an economic power because of their new-found values and willing sacrifice. An interesting by-product of this process is that South Korea is taking much of the electronic market from Japan. In addition, some of the best computers, automobiles, and modern goods are built by this new and growing work force. South Korea will soon have a per capita income comparable to the West and will be a major exporter to the rest of the world.

In 1986, when South Korea began reunification talks with North Korea, a parade was held in Seoul. Dignitaries from the North were riding with delegates from the South when their vehicles were detained in a traffic jam. One of the South Korean officials apologized for the traffic delay.

"You cannot fool us," one of the North Koreans smirked, "You wanted to impress us with your capitalistic success so you obviously had these automobiles brought in to deceive us! But you cannot fool us--bringing in all these cars was too *easy*."

The South Korean host looked out at the city and smiled. "Yes, you are right," he said. "Bringing in the autos *was easy*--what was really difficult was bringing in all those skyscrapers and factories!"

South Korea stands today as an amazing illustration of God's blessing resulting from a tremendous spiritual Awakening. This Awakening has genuinely influenced an entire culture--with political, economic, cultural, and religious effects. Korea is now experiencing its--

FIRST GREAT AWAKENING.

China: The Largest Nation in the World

To most people China is the "sleeping giant," a land of deep mystery and paradox. For most of our lifetime, China has been closed to the West, and the news media has seen little and reported less. However, as the nation with the largest population (with over one billion people), China has long held an attraction for the West.

China was one of the first countries to benefit from the world missions thrust of the previous Great Awakenings. J. Hudson Taylor is the legendary missionary to China. Taylor buried two wives and several children while opening China to the Gospel during the late 1800's. Despite his sacrificial and diligent labor, there were but 75,000 professing Christians in China by 1900. From this relatively small base, the number of believers grew to three million by 1949, with a strong and stable church.

Then Mao took over China and began a reign of terror and persecution against landowners, political rightists, and Christians. Thousands of believers were martyred as Mao killed perhaps as many as 30 million Chinese--more people than Hitler and Stalin combined.

By 1979, thirty years after the Communist takeover of China, only an estimated one-million Christians survived. Yet,miraculously, in 1979 the churches were permitted to reopen and the church buildings and facilities (which had been confiscated by Mao and used for government or public purposes) were returned to the churches.

The churches, by government decree, were only permitted to practice their faith within the walls of the church buildings. Even though only "approved" pastors were permitted to preach and teach, and no identifying denominational or group "label" other than "Christian" was permitted, this was still an amazing change. After 30 years of terror, repression, and persecution, God had obviously worked in the hearts of the Chinese leaders to permit an oriental equivalent to *glasnost*.

In 1982 I visited mainland China two times (just three years after the relaxation of restrictions on the Christian church). Our tour group traveled to Shanghai, Xian, Canton, Qualing, and Beijing to visit churches and to discuss with government officials the English language and Christian education.

Every one of the churches I visited was packed to overflowing, and the buildings reverberated to the glorious sounds of the music and preaching of the Gospel. There was an openness everywhere, and I had the privilege of leading some of our Communist guides to Christ.

This awakening was definitely not a Western movement. All missionaries were expelled or killed shortly after Mao invaded in 1949. The churches had been closed and all preachers who did not co-operate had been tortured or killed. Those who returned to secular work were placed in vocation assignments. Christianity went underground.

When the government permitted the churches to reopen in 1979, the pastors were forced to put aside their differences, and all denominational labels were outlawed. The consensus of the pastors (all over 70 years of age) was orthodoxy. They were required to cooperate and to "stick to the fundamentals," and they could not teach denominational distinctives. Thus, the awakening in China is a basic (literal) Fundamental Biblical Orthodoxy with a uniting of the faith that was overwhelming to me. I asked the 78-year-old pastor in Shenzhen, "How would you accept me as a member of your church?" (He had been a Wesleyan years ago.)

His response through the interpreter was, "If you confess that you have trusted Jesus Christ as your Savior and that your sin has been forgiven and you have been baptized (by immersion), you could join our church."

The national church is still on its own, though not quite alone. God's Holy Spirit is with the Chinese Christian leaders. Today, a new church is opening every day inside mainland China. *Tens of thousands* of house churches are scattered all over the nation, and 12 new seminaries have started for the training of Christian workers (in 1982 there was only one Christian seminary, with 40 students).

In 1986 Dr. James Hudson Taylor, great-grandson of the missions pioneer who opened China, reported that the Church in China was exploding. The estimates are that more than *50 million Chinese now profess Jesus Christ as Savior*. In just *seven years* of experiencing its own Awakening, the Church in China has almost caught up with the American Church!

It is astounding to consider that "atheistic" China has printed 1.6 million Bibles in the Chinese language since 1980. The new openness toward Christianity in China was perhaps well illustrated in 1988 when Billy Graham was permitted to preach in churches all across China. Chinese leaders in Hong Kong agree that this country may have *100 million* Christians by the year 2000.

Pastor Ingram of First Assembly of God Church of Palmer, Texas, recounted that Thomas Zimmerman, Superintendent of the Assemblies of God, stated in the denomination magazine that the Nazarene churches in mainland China were experiencing miracles like a chapter out of the book of Acts. A leader of the Nazarene U.S. church wrote him a letter stating that this was not true. A short time later the Nazarene leader visited China, and in a letter of apology to Dr. Zimmerman, he confirmed that miracles were indeed being experienced in China. China is experiencing its--

FIRST GREAT AWAKENING.

The second most populous nation in the world is China's neighbor to the south. India has some 800 million people and is growing at over 1.3 million *every month.*

India, although a democracy, is basically a Hindu nation. The Hindu religion dominates its culture to such an extent that it has been difficult to reach typical Indians with the Gospel. Muslims have also made inroads throughout India. Christianity is dubbed "the white man's religion" with strong ties to the old colonialism, and has traditionally been unpopular.

For years Christianity has been strongest in the state of Kerola in southwestern India. Tradition says that the Apostle Thomas came here following the resurrection of Jesus. Over the years, the Christian church in Kerola has become quite institutionalized and appears to have little of the evangelical message intact.

The northeast frontier area of India, near the Burma-China borders, is inhabited by hill and jungle tribes whose religions were related to headhunting as recently as 1900. The British colonial rulers had great troubles with these 1.5 million headhunters and in 1906 lost 500 lives in a single massacre at a tea plantation.

In 1908 a revival broke out in Wales, and a young Welsh pharmacist by the name of Watkin Roberts was converted. At the age of 23, Roberts left Wales for Northeast India. Roberts lived among the tribespeople and led five young Hmar men to the Lord before the British made him leave. One of these converts was Chawnga (pronounced Chonga) of the clan of Pudaite. He was a son of the chief.

Chawnga memorized the Gospel of John (written in the language of a neighboring tribe, as the

Hmars had no written language) left by Missionary Roberts, and he began to share his faith. He started a church--the first in Northeast India--and became its pastor. He taught his children God's ways. His son, Rochunga, "gave his name to Jesus" at age ten. The boy walked 90 miles through jungles to go to school and learn English. He then attended a mission high school some 150 miles away, after which he received a scholarship to attend Allabahad University in Calcutta. The young man, Rochunga, next studied at the University of Edinburgh in Scotland and then Wheaton College in America.

Rochunga translated the New Testament from Greek into a written language he had created for his people in India, the Hmar tribe. Hundreds of schools and churches were established so the people could learn to read and write and study God's Word in their own language.

As a result of Watkin Robert's first five converts to Christianity and the later work of Rochunga Pudaite and other Hmar Christian leaders, 75 to 80 percent of all the people in Northeast India are now professing Christians: the Hmar tribe, 90 percent; the Khasis tribe, 67 percent; the Naga tribe, 90 percent; the Mizo tribe, 98 percent. The work is now reaching out into other regions of that area, including the 1.5 million population of Tripura state, where Meitei Hindus have become open to the Gospel.

Another Indian leader, David Jesudas of Northeast India, focuses his work on securing abandoned children; he raises capital from churches in the United States in order to care for these children. Mr. Jesudas feeds and clothes them and provides Christian schools to "disciple" them into Christian leaders.

As young K. P. Yohannan ministered in southern India in 1982, churches were established in 21 villages in just three months time. He took the

Gospel to Jaipur in western India, where, under his preaching, over 1000 were converted to Christ in a week. Yohannan saw this as the beginning of an Awakening he had prayed for since 1971.

That same area of India has seen an unusual outpouring of God's Spirit in the last ten years. Indian believers estimate the number of new Christians to be between 10 and 15 million in the area of Rajasthan alone.

John Gollapalli preaches on three radio stations in India. One station, which is located in Sri Lanka, reaches almost all of India. Brother Gollapalli receives an average of 8000 letters a month from inquiring Hindu listeners wanting to know more about Christ.

Christianity is growing at such a rate in India that many Hindus are asking the government to pass restrictions on its growth. After the British gave India its independence on August 15, 1947, the new government issued no new missionary visas. However, about 1500 Western missionaries already living in India were permitted to stay by renewing their visas. In December 1986 the government passed a new policy that no missionary visas would be renewed. Although India has freedom of religion, the Hindus are on the defensive and quite concerned about conversions to Christianity.

During this decade A.M.G. and its leader Spiros Zodhiates (called "The Greek") began presenting the Gospel in a new way to the people of India. Gospel ads were placed in 120 secular magazines and newspapers with a high profile all over India. The response to these ads runs an average of 35,000 to 50,000 a week from Hindus and Muslims desiring to know Christ.

There is equal success in the growing Christian school movement across India. The English language, although second to Hindi in India, is the language of commerce, and proficiency in English is coveted by Indians to ensure success in the world. As a result, Christian schools are popular not only among believers for their own youngsters, but are also popular among Hindus, Muslims, and even Communists who line up to enroll their children in Christian schools in order for them to learn English. Also, the quality of education is expected to be better in the Christian schools than in the government schools.

Christian schools are becoming tools for evangelism in India. Rochunga Pudaite reports that when he starts a Christian school in his area, a church soon follows. The goal he has set is for Christian school teachers and principals to become the *"new gurus"* to bring Christianity to over 100,000 Indian villages. Accelerated Christian Education already has several warehouses of used curriculum in India, with more than 50 schools on the A.C.E. program.

I have seen this growing openness first-hand during many visits which I have made to India since 1976. For example, in a small meeting in Bombay where I was addressing church and Christian school leaders on how to start a school, I noticed a young man. During a break I asked, "Are you a Christian teacher?"

"No," he replied politely. "I am a Muslim. I have attended the university and am interested in education."

"How did you happen to visit us?" I asked.

"I am attending at the invitation of the pastor's son," the Muslim answered.

"Have *you* ever thought about becoming a Christian?" I asked him.

To my surprise, he nodded affirmatively and said, "Yes, I have."

I showed him my Bible. "Do you believe the Bible is the Word of God?"

Again he answered, "Yes."

"Do you believe that you are a sinner?"

"Yes . . ."

(I asked myself, "What am I doing wrong; surely he doesn't understand!")

I continued through questions designed to present the plan of salvation and discovered his interest was keen and his spiritual hunger was genuine. He acknowledged his sin and his belief in Jesus Christ as the Son of God and in His atoning death and resurrection. He expressed his belief that God through Christ would save him from his sins.

Eagerly he knelt beside his friend, the son of the pastor, and prayed in repentance, receiving Christ as Savior. Everyone at the meeting rejoiced.

I have personally witnessed this same kind of sincere spiritual hunger all over India. The nation is "ripe unto harvest," and God is visiting India with its--

FIRST GREAT AWAKENING.

Russia

The third largest country in the world is the U.S.S.R. Actually, with *eleven* time zones and the world's greatest land area, the Soviet Union would be considered the largest country. Its population of about 300 million people has been under Communist rule since the October 1917 revolution. Under Stalinist purges and continuing persecution, the Christian Church has had an extremely difficult time behind the Iron Curtain.

Yet Russia--like China--seems to be showing signs that the government is shifting to the right. This may be our clue that a revival, a reform, or an Awakening might be taking place in Russia and the rest of the Soviet Union.

Since the mid-1970's, Bibles for the World has sent over 600,000 Russian Bibles into the U.S.S.R. through a cultural exchange agreement between Russia and India.

The Orthodox Church has now printed over 100,000 Bibles and has imported another 100,000. The Institute for Bible Translation in Stockholm has completed a reprint of the *Tolkovaya Bibliya*. This is a prerevolutionary edition of the Russian Bible (printed from 1904 to 1914) with a commentary by Lopukhin. Ten thousand copies of the three-volume set have been printed for distribution among Christians in Russia.

In 1972 the United States and the U.S.S.R. reached a temporary agreement to freeze ICBM's at their then current levels and to cooperate in other areas. This *detente* paved the way for Gorbachev's *glasnost* or *perestroika* of recent years. Reagan-Gorbachev agreements on nuclear weapons and the pullout of Soviet troops from Afghanistan are bearing fruit.

During the past ten years, the Soviets have allowed some 130,000 Jews and over 40,000 others to emigrate from the U.S.S.R. In May 1988 the Soviets allowed the Western news media to film a formerly forbidden activity--an opposition political meeting. For the first time since 1917 when all but the Communist party were prohibited, Russians had formed a "democratic" party to oppose Communism. Several Eastern block countries permitted Billy Graham to preach in recent years, and paradoxically, one Soviet satellite nation, Poland, even provided the world's current Roman Catholic leader, Pope John Paul II.

Please note that in no country do I necessarily equate their religion with true Bible faith. Neither do I acknowledge any specific kind of religious faith as Bible Christianity. However, I do believe that Fundamental, Bible Faith is at the heart of this present religious Awakening and is its prime influence.

Glasnost has apparently helped pave the way for greater religious freedom and growth in the U.S.S.R. The Soviets claim that Bibles and religious materials are now permitted inside Russia. For the first time in history, the Russian Orthodox Church was given "prime time" for nationwide television coverage of the Resurrection story at Easter.

Word has also leaked out to the West that the Russian Orthodox Church is experiencing spiritual renewal; so are Baptists, Lutherans, Pentecostals, and "unregistered" or underground churches. Christianity has exploded in the *gulags* and concentration camps across Russia. Now, even government leaders and the Russian youth are being won to Christ.

Dr. Dennis Brindley, a conservative Baptist pastor from Oregon, reported that one of his missionaries, Mical Newman from Madagascar, told him of the Awakening he was seeing in this socialistic island-state off the east coast of Africa. The missionary related that the state sends its brightest and most hopeful young men to Europe and Russia for training in government operations. He said that those who go to France return hardened Communists and that those who go to Russia for training returned to Madagascar as evangelical Christians.

Alexander Solzhenitsyn has said it is likely that *one-third* of the Russian population is Christian. (Communist party membership in 1978 was reported to be just over 16 million.) House churches are springing up everywhere and a great lay evangelism movement is taking place. Best estimates say there are *at least 50 million believers* in the U.S.S.R. Others say the number of professing Christians in the Soviet Union *could be more than 100 million*--that is over 33 percent of the nation.

Glasnost is an expression of liberty now being tested and practiced in the Soviet Union, perhaps in direct response to a host of praying believers who put into practice the promise of II Chronicles 7:14, "If my people, which are called by my name, shall humble themselves, and pray, and seek my face, and turn from their wicked ways; then, will I hear from heaven, and will forgive their sin, and will heal their land."

What great and refreshing news to learn that Russia is now experiencing its--

FIRST GREAT AWAKENING.

United States

The United States is the fourth largest country in the world. We have already seen how God has brought a Great Awakening to America since 1970, with 40 percent of Americans confessing faith in Christ--its Third Great Awakening.

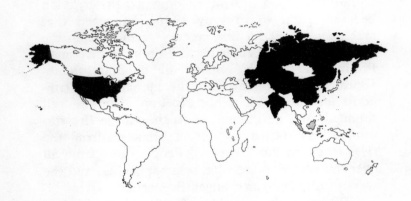

Indonesia

The fifth largest nation is Indonesia, with 150 million people living on a chain of 13,000 islands north of Australia, south of China, and west of India (in Southeast Asia). These islands are in an ocean area some 1500 miles wide and 3000 miles long--and would just about fit into the land area of the United States.

Three hundred years ago--a generation after the Pilgrims settled in America--Dutch Presbyterians first took the Gospel to Indonesia. However, until 1965 (almost three centuries later) very little had happened in the spread of the Gospel in Indonesia. By 1961, an independent, indigenous Christian church existed on the islands, but claimed only about 30,000 members, mostly in central Java.

In September 1965 the Indonesian government, under President Sukarno, was threatened by a Communist insurgent takeover. The newspapers of the West explained how the Muslims averted the coup, protected Indonesia, and preserved the nation from Communism.

On September 16, 1965, just four days before the attempted Communist coup, in the village of Soe on the island of Timor, some 200 Presbyterian believers gathered to pray. What happened that evening reads like a first century account from the book of Acts. As people began to pray in that small Presbyterian church, outside the building, flames appeared to be coming from the church, and it triggered an immediate public reaction. The fire bell sounded, and neighbors ran to the village fire station; others started a "bucket brigade" from the river to douse the "flames." People came from all over the village to see what was happening, and the service turned into an evangelistic meeting.

By midnight a thousand of the people had turned to Christ. This was only a beginning. The intervention of God prevented the Communist coup and prepared the country for the "mighty wind" of revival and conversion that has swept across Indonesia for 20 years. Today, *23 million Muslims have professed Christ as Savior in Indonesia.* The Christian Missionary Alliance Church now has more church members in Indonesia than in the United States. It is reported that the latest census of the nation is being withheld because the statistics in favor of Christians would embarrass the Muslim-controlled government.

A young jungle boy, Melchoir Tari, was in the Presbyterian church that September night when the fire of God fell. The experience not only changed his life, but that of his nation. Mel Tari was commissioned by God to carry a message to Christians in America: "Get back to the simplicity of the

Word of God."

He did not speak English, had no money, knew nothing about American culture, but felt a strong urgency to bring that message to the U.S. Mel Tari did not know that Americans, while their coins declared "In God We Trust," had been affected by the humanism of its educational system.

Our Western humanist mindset has conditioned us to rationalize away much of the Bible and its teaching. Affluence, heated denominational divisions, and Western "Laodiceanism" have made it difficult to believe and expect God's power for Awakening. God sent a "missionary" from Indonesia to preach the message: "Get back to the simplicity of God's Word."

Mr. Tari had his first opportunity to come to the U.S. in 1969. However, as strange as it sounds, God told him "No--you are to go in 1970." Indonesia's FIRST GREAT AWAKENING began in 1965, but the next Great Awakening in the United States was not to begin until 1970.

In Indonesia, the Great Awakening continues. In 1979 a native Indonesian, Cris Marantika, organized the Evangelical Theological Seminary of Java. His group has also opened some 327 churches and started "branch" seminaries to train Indonesian Christians. Their goal is to establish a church in each of the islands' 50,000 villages by the year 2015.

A.M.G. will establish over 1000 churches in Indonesia by 1990. These churches will all be composed of Muslim converts.

Indonesia is in the midst of its--

FIRST GREAT AWAKENING.

China, India, Russia, the United States, and Indonesia are the five largest nations in the world. Add Korea, and these six nations alone represent 2.78 billion people, or just over one-half of the world's population. These nations are already experiencing the impact of spiritual awakening.

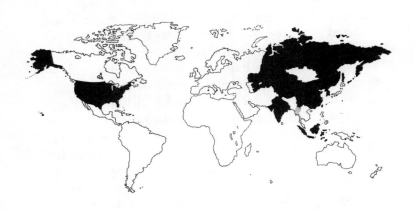

Burma

By 1965 missionaries had been expelled from Burma, but this has had little effect on the growth of Christianity there. The churches in Burma continue to grow.

In Kachin, a region in northern Burma near the Indo-China border, there are more than 100,000 Baptist believers. In 1977, in celebration of the Baptist Centennial Convention, Burmese Christians baptized some 6000 new converts--twice the number who were saved on the day of Pentecost (Acts 2:41). Reports also tell of widespread conversions to Christianity among the military ranks and leadership in Burma.

This country is typical of what God is doing in Southeast Asia as He pours out His Spirit. The harvest is ripe.

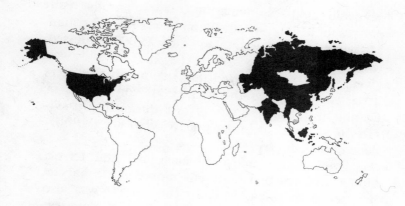

Cambodia

The Viet Nam war ravaged the small nation of Cambodia, a country the size of Missouri, with a little over six million people. Cambodia (or Kampuchea) has been embroiled in conflict for nearly a quarter of a century. When Khmer Rouge forces captured Phnom Penh in 1975, over 100,000 had died in five years of fighting. During the 70's, over one million people (one-sixth of the population) were killed in executions, forced hardships, and genocide. Thousands of refugees tried to flee to Thailand. The ones who did escape had to face possible starvation and the breakup and loss of families. It was a terrible period of terror and tribulation.

However, this period was also a time of an outpouring of God's love. Humanitarian aid, in the form of food and medicine, was allowed in 1979 to help the famine-stricken country and its helpless people. This aid was often accompanied by Christian compassion and generosity. Organizations with an evangelical Christian perspective and purpose were permitted to help with the humanitarian work among the refugees.

During this period of massive upheaval and

genocide, God's Spirit began to work, and the people responded in massive numbers. The Christian Missionary Alliance counted some 25,000 professed converts just during the first year that aid was given. The CMA reported that this number of converts was *five times* the number of conversions in Cambodia through CMA efforts during the *previous 50 years* of missionary activity within the borders of that country.

Even in the midst of such evil and terror, God's love reached out, and more of the harvest has begun to ripen. In *Laos* the harvest was also ripe. Thousands of refugees from the Viet Nam war fled to the West, aided by Western Christians.

In Australia and America, where most of the Laotian refugees settled, new believers among the Laotians are building churches in numbers that will no doubt surpass the number of Buddhist temples being built.

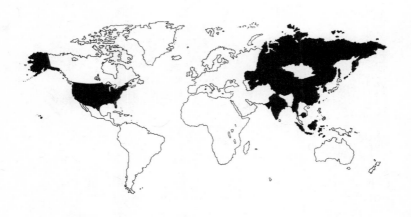

Philippines

This country of nearly 60 million people consists, like Indonesia, of a number of islands. The Philippine Islands were conquered by Spain over

300 years ago. The Catholic Church has since dominated the Philippine culture. Each city and every *barrio* has a Roman Catholic church.

The Catholic churches, however, are not like those in America. The "Black Virgin" is worshiped and strange practices are observed. Every year people whip themselves in self-flagellation until their bodies are torn and bloody. Then they fall into the dirt and the salt water along the beaches to do penance. Every year at least one person allows others to nail him to a cross to demonstrate his personal piety and to celebrate religious festivities.

Some traditional churches had a heavy emphasis on superstition, which continued even through the Japanese occupation of the Philippines during World War II. It was after the war that the Gospel was introduced by evangelical Protestant missionaries, when there were only eight million Filipinos.

Today, with the population more than seven times what it was in post-World War II days, the country wavers between a Communist revolution and an experiment in democracy. But the most significant events in the Philippines do not make news headlines. The growth of Bible-believing churches in the Philippines seems to be passing even the rate of population growth. All over the 7100 Philippine Islands churches are opening.

As more and more churches are started, Christian schools are also opening. More than 150 A.C.E. schools are now in operation in the Philippines, training its future leaders and Christian workers.

Outside observers are impressed with the results of A.C.E. schools upon the traditionally matriarchal society. The schools are making positive changes in the families as well as raising the educational level. A.C.E. places an emphasis on the family, especially on the need for the father to assume the leadership in the religious and educational needs of his family. The A.C.E. school system is approved by the government and encouraged by the Office of Education in Manila.

President Aquino (who has declared her own Christian faith) has met with evangelical and Fundamentalist leaders from the U.S. In February 1988 she met with Dr. Brad Weniger, President of the Baptist Bible Fellowship of California; Dr. Wally Beebe; Art Sims; and Philippine nationals, as part of the International Fundamental Baptist Congress. The historic meeting was given wide press coverage in Manila.

American Christians serve as Mrs. Aquino's advisors on matters of church and the growth of Christianity in the Philippines. There is one group of pastors and evangelists who visit the Philippines regularly. One of the evangelists in this group tours the islands on each visit and, with permission from the government, conducts Gospel meetings in the public high schools. He gives invitations and passes out tracts and Bibles. Thousands respond on each tour he makes of the islands.

The World Awakening harvest is taking place here, where already 92 percent of the population is said to be Christian, including the Catholics--some in name only--with an unknown number of true believers who are committed to changing their nation for God.

Latin America

The 20 nations of Latin America stretch from the U.S.A. border, through Mexico and Central and South America, to the Straits of Magellan at the bottom of the world near Antarctica. Most of the original Latin American settlers were Indians, probably Semitic people from Asia who came across the Aleutian Islands into the Americas about the time of the reign of King David.

Two significant Indian cultures, the Maya and Inca tribes, had spread throughout Latin America by the time the Spanish explorers came. These Spanish explorers were Catholic and "converted" the Indians by the sword. Many of the Indians of South and Central America were wiped out by the military superiority of the white men or by the white man's diseases.

The Catholic Church became the dominant force in Latin culture, and millions of Indians, plus Spanish and Portuguese settlers, retained the Catholic religion. In 1900 there were only 50,000 acknowledged evangelical Christians in all of these Latin countries.

But by the 1930's, there were a million--

By the 1940's, there were two million--

By the 1950's, some five million--

By the 1960's, ten million--

At this time there are an estimated 20 to 40 million professing evangelical Christians in Latin America, and it is predicted there will be 100 million by 2000 A.D.

The majority of these Christians will be Pentecostals. In one country of Central America, the Assembly of God denomination alone has an annual growth rate of 44 percent. Latin America is experiencing its--

FIRST GREAT AWAKENING.

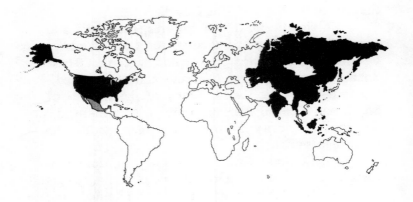

Mexico

What is happening just south of the United States border was not expected. The Catholic nation of Mexico has been the object of border missions since the turn of the century, but "bread and the Gospel missions" from the U.S. were the main successful movements in the poverty-stricken villages where the priest ruled the constituents without competition.

Today Bible-believing churches are springing up everywhere among the nationals. The two largest national denominations are Full Gospel Church of God and the Assemblies of God, and are found in all states. King's Castle is a new movement that appears to be strictly a Mexican national church. By the mid-80's the total number of evangelical churches had risen to between 10,000 and 15,000 and claimed 10 percent of the Mexican people--and the number is still growing.

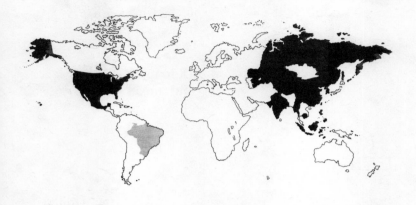

Brazil

What is happening in Brazil is typical of what is happening throughout South America. Brazil has *six million* Assembly of God members alone. One church, in Sao Paulo, has 25,000 members. The size of its building is staggering. When it was being built, someone asked, "How many pews are being purchased?"

The reply was, "One and one-half *miles*!"

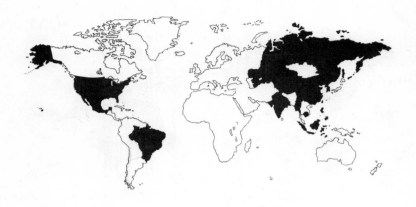

Chile

This country is also experiencing explosive Christian growth. There is a great deal of open-air street preaching. In the United States such presentations of the Gospel would likely be ignored or ridiculed--but in Chile, street evangelism is highly effective.

Church growth has brought unusual problems. In Santiago, the capital of Chile, the sanctuary of one Methodist Pentecostal church will seat 16,000; but nearly 90,000 members want to attend worship! Church leaders have asked its members to attend worship services only once a month and at other times to attend smaller neighborhood Bible classes. This Santiago church has a 1000-voice choir and a music group with 1000 mandolins.

The Andes

A mountain range of 5000 miles extends from Colombia (just north of the equator) through Ecuador, Peru, Chile, and Argentina. These mountains, known as the Andes, are home to 100 thousand Quichua Indians.

Originally, Christianity made slow gains among the Quichua tribes. From 1945 to 1970 only about 300 converts were recorded. However, the Gospel Missionary Union, working among the Quichuas, reported that in the 1970's the Quichua church had grown to 30,000, and by the 1980's was over 50,000.

The Quichua church is made up primarily of peasant farmers. These simple people are willing to walk for days, over unbelievably difficult mountain terrain, to share the Gospel with other Quichua Indians.

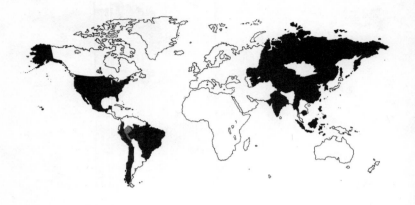

Peru

Christian Missionary Alliance and LeTourneau Foundation have started three churches in Lima that already have over 2000 members each. Many pastors in Peru have a real interest in a quality education for their young people, and they have turned to A.C.E. to help them start Christian schools. Even the government of Peru is interested and is willing to talk about ways A.C.E. can help the entire nation with its educational needs.

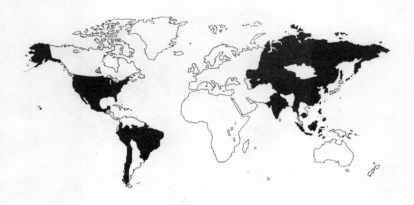

Guatemala

Like Peru, Guatemala is interested in establishing A.C.E. schools. In 1975 (when I first visited that country) Guatemala was 96 percent Roman Catholic and four percent Protestant evangelical. Just eight years later, in 1983, the ratio had shifted dramatically to 72 percent Catholic, 28 percent evangelical.

Pastor Jose Munoz from Guatemala City reports that his church now has over 4,000 members and a large Christian school. He believes the number of evangelicals in Guatemala is now well over 30 percent.

Southern Baptists have a work among the Kekchis Indians. This Southern Baptist work had 225 members in 1972; the number was over 2000 by 1980.

Christian schools have exploded in Guatemala as evangelical believers attempt to retrieve their children from government schools dominated by Roman Catholic influence.

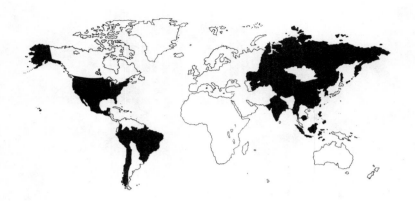

El Salvador

In the capital city of San Salvador, *Centro Evangelistico* is a growing evangelical church which usually has some 15,000 people in attendance each Sunday. The Communist influence of terror in El Salvador has prompted a turning to Christ. Churches are growing in every part of the country. Five Christian schools have now been established.

Christianity Today (January 15, 1988) reports, "Latin America's conservative Protestant churches have experienced phenomenal growth, increasing from an estimated 5000 in 1900, to upwards of 40 million today. In this predominantly Catholic region, one-tenth of the population is now Protestant . . . . Some leaders say the Latin American Church--given the needed tools and training--could move to the forefront of world evangelism."

The magazine also reported on the recent *Ibero-American* Missions Congress (COMIBAM) which attracted over 2700 evangelical delegates from 23 Latin nations. According to missionary authority Ralph Winter, "COMIBAM represented the first time in history that churches in the Third World, through their own initiative, have met to discuss the fulfillment of the Great Commission."

God could by-pass the affluent, rational humanistic Laodicean church of the West during this end-time harvest. He has plenty of churches less affected who are catching the vision for world evangelization.

The evangelical and fundamentalist churches of at least eight Latin countries, including several already mentioned, recognize the relationship of education to evangelism. Marxist nations send promising youth to Cuba or Russia for education as teachers, journalists, and other kinds of leaders. But a growing number of leaders are interested in providing more of the young people with a quality education, and hence the interest in A.C.E.

In December 1987, at the invitation of the Vice President of the *Dominican Republic*, Christian leaders met with the Secretary of State, the Minister of Education, and another cabinet official. All of these officials expressed an openness toward the A.C.E. educational system and even its Theistic curriculum. Government leaders in Latin America say that they want God in education and see the possibility of some kind of cooperative venture to provide quality education for all the children.

The Bible is becoming so popular in many Latin countries that it is sold in markets and department stores. Catholics are turning to Jesus Christ in repentance and in search of a personal relationship with the Savior. Latin America is now experiencing its--

FIRST GREAT AWAKENING

Africa

British explorers referred to Africa as the "dark continent." Its civilization had been by-passed by that of the Western world, and most of the African tribes were animistic and believed in a simplistic system of evil spirits and witch doctors. It was to these basically superstitious tribal cultures that missionaries were called in the eighteenth and nineteenth centuries. British missionaries like David Livingston opened Africa to the Gospel, Christian faith, and trade.

By that time, Islam had already spread throughout many of the African nations, and it was not until the twentieth century that Christianity began to sweep across Africa with any significance. Two centuries of sacrificial and dedicated missionary activity produced some 7 million professed Christians in Africa by 1900.

This number of Christians increased by 50 percent during the next 75 years. By 1976 there were 15 million professing Christians in Africa. This growth mainly resulted from successful African work by missionaries from America and Great Britain.

The truly astounding news is what has taken place in Africa in *just the last 12 years*. Close examination of the facts point to events of startling significance. Today, the best estimates indicate there are now between *150 and 200 million professing Christians in Africa*. Some estimates say that by the year 2000 there will be *400 million African Christians* (A.M.G. states that 50 percent of the African population already profess to be born again).

During this century the Christian population of Africa has increased dramatically--from nine percent (in 1900) to an expected 48 percent (in A.D. 2000). Most of that explosive growth has taken place in just the last decade.

Perhaps no other continent so obviously reflects the significance of this global event of Awakening as Africa. Africa is now experiencing its--

FIRST GREAT AWAKENING.

Zaire

Formerly the Belgian Congo, Zaire became independent in 1960, and in 1964 became a "People's Republic." The country became the Republic of Zaire in 1971. The next year, Zairians with Christian names were ordered to adopt African names.

Zaire has known strife, persecution, and political corruption since its independence. Nevertheless, God's Spirit has touched this nation of 30 million people.

By 1986 the new African Independent Church Movement had about 6000 new church groups. Today, a new denominational group is forming every day in Zaire. The Christian church is active and is growing significantly, with 70 percent of Zaire now professing Christians.

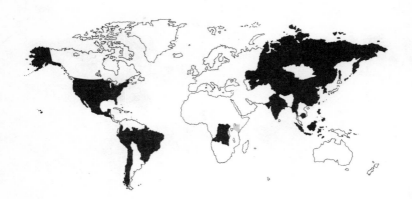

Kenya

This nation of 20 million won independence from Britain in 1963 and developed a private enterprise system. Kenya has enjoyed a relatively free political life and has a good tradition of ties to Christianity. Protestant and Catholic missionaries have made an impact on the country with schools, hospitals, and churches.

In recent years the traditional forms of religion have been shaken. Catholics in Kenya have split from Rome over the Bible. One Kenyan church leader says, "Everything we do, we do according to the Bible."

Today the Catholic church in Kenya more closely resembles an evangelical, Protestant church--with heavy emphasis on "Gospel preaching" according to a New Testament style. The congregation is active, acting in obedience to the simple preaching of the Bible. None of the clergy draws a salary, and they live by Biblical patterns of simplicity and faith.

A number of Kenya's political leaders are professing Christians, and churches are sprouting all over Nairobi (with a population of 1.1 million), as well as throughout hundreds of villages.

Christianity is alive and well in Kenya.

Nigeria

This country, the largest on the African continent, is more than twice the size of California. The majority of the Nigerian population (103 million) are Muslim.

A generation ago, Nigeria's government ruled that an animistic tribe would receive an elementary education and that religion would be taught as part of the curriculum. Parents in this tribe were asked to choose between the Koran (Islam) and the Bible (Christianity). The tribe's hatred for Islam was stronger than their indifference to Christianity. They chose the Bible, and this book has had a dramatic influence on the younger generation.

New church planters are having the greatest time in West African history. One black native evangelist has helped establish 258 churches just during the past five years. Another church-planting evangelist says, "There is such a turning to Christ that we are not able to keep up with baptisms of new converts."

Archbishop Benson Idahosa's organization, *World Outreach Centre*, is located in Muslim-dominated Nigeria where the group witnesses a great harvest of souls. Idahosa has started some

3000 churches in Nigeria alone. He also trains pastors, evangelists, and Christian workers to take the Gospel elsewhere ("the uttermost part of the earth.")

Idahosa's own church, in Benin City, Nigeria, *seats 30,000*. His evangelistic crusades draw people by the *tens of thousands*. The meetings are attended by throngs of people--with as many as *200,000* in some crusades. In Lagos, Nigeria, in 1985 one of Benson Idahosa's meetings was described as "the crusade of the century," with an estimated one million in attendance *each night*.

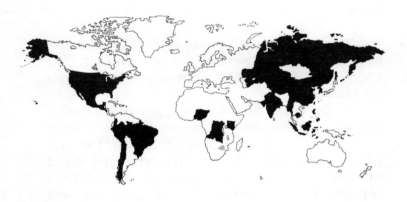

Zimbabwe

Zimbabwe (a small country formerly known as Rhodesia) achieved independence in 1980 following a revolution by the black majority to wrest control of the government from the white minority. Robert Mugabe became Prime Minister after the revolution.

Zimbabwe has seen an unusual surge of Christianity. Church growth--which took place in spite of internal strife and opposition--has been a significant event in Zimbabwe. One church planter has started over 240 new churches during the past ten years.

It is both exciting and perplexing to see people coming to Christ by the tens of thousands. It is perplexing to the Western mind because of its training in rational humanism and its conditioning to believe that unless we send missionaries and work among the people, evangelism is impossible.

God is working spontaneously today in Central Africa, in the same way He is pouring out His Spirit upon Indonesia, China, and India.

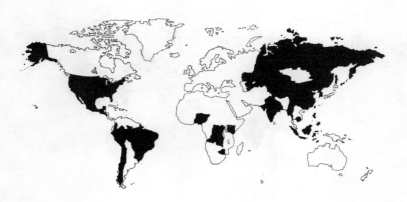

Uganda

Ugandan General Idi Amin grabbed power from Prime Minister Milton Obote in 1971. His coup was followed by terror and a blood bath. At least *one-third of a million people* were massacred by Amin. Historian Paul Johnson reports that Amin even killed his own wife, keeping her remains in a freezer and engaging in cannibalism.

Many church leaders were martyred during this period of rampant evil in Uganda. Christians by the thousands were tortured, raped, mutilated, and machine-gunned. Economic and social chaos brought even further hardship, famine, and terror.

Still, Christianity was not extinguished. In fact, although Idi Amin (and subsequent Communist attempts to destroy or control the government) left a nation of poverty-stricken pilgrims and internal refugees, the Church came back stronger than ever. Evangelists from neighboring Tanzania, Kenya, and Zaire brought the good news of the Gospel. Inside the country, surviving pastors and evangelists continued to turn the nation to Christ.

Ethiopia

Ethiopia has been a Marxist nation since 1975, although the country traces its Christian roots to A.D. 330 when the Coptic (orthodox) church began.

Since 1972 a series of severe droughts has caused widespread famines which have devastated the country--*hundreds of thousands* have died from starvation. Extended drought reached its worst in 1984. A world-wide relief effort focused attention on millions of Ethiopians facing starvation and death.

A civil war of over 27 years between the Marxist government in the capital, Addis Ababa, and the separatist rebels in the north has only added to the people's grief, suffering, and despair. The U.S. State Department predicted that another *two million people would starve* in 1988 (*U.S. News and World Report*, April 15, 1988).

Ethiopia was 40 percent Christian and 40 percent Muslim when the Marxists took over. Despite bloody coups, persecution, and terror, the Church not only has survived, *but has flourished*. The people are turning to Christ *en masse*.

Sudan Interior Missions (SIM) is said to be starting *one new church each week* in Ethiopia. Even during severe persecution, the *Lutheran Church*, which had 30,000 members in 1960, grew to 100,000 by 1978. Then, amazingly, the Lutherans increased their membership to five times as many in just two years (1978 to 1980)--to some 500,000.

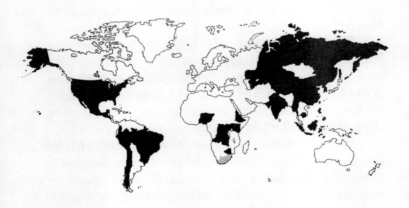

South Africa

During World War II, a German father serving in the military was separated from his wife and four-year-old son. The mother and boy were miraculously saved from death on at least two occasions during the terrible events of the war. The family was finally reunited after the fighting ended.

The family was Christian and attended an Assembly of God church, where the boy was converted. Later, he attended a "faith" Bible college in England, where he was called to the mission field.

Young Reinhard Bonnke went as a missionary to the tiny country of *Lesotho* (formerly Basutoland) with a population of 1.5 million people. Bonnke was not content to have a standard missionary influence, so he spent long hours in prayer before God seeking His power for effective change in Africa.

As a result of Bonnke's prayer, important changes occurred in his ministry. As an evangelist, he had been seeing hundreds come to his meetings; now, thousands began to attend. Spurred by this evidence of God's power, Reinhard Bonnke's prayer life took on a single focus: "Africa shall be saved!"

To accommodate the large crowds, Bonnke had a tent built for his evangelistic crusades. The tent was the largest ever to be built and took five years to construct. It required 14 semi-trailer trucks to haul it, took eight weeks to erect it, and was seven stories tall when erected.

Since "open-air meetings" were prohibited by law in many countries of southern Africa, Bonnke's huge tent was an answer as to how to speak to massive crowds. The tent could seat up to 30,000, and if the people stood, it could accommodate 70,000. By 1986, the evangelist's meetings drew crowds of 80,000 to 100,000, and the huge tent was too small!

Reinhard Bonnke joined Nigerian evangelist Benson Idahosa in 1986 to conduct what was probably the largest evangelistic crusade ever conducted in a Muslim city. Newspapers reported that 500,000 people attended.

Entire villages, with their populations of 80,000 to 100,000, are coming to Christ. *Every month, hundreds of thousands are accepting Jesus Christ as Savior* throughout Africa in Bonnke crusades. In his crusades about 1.5 million people sign decision cards every year, acknowledging faith in Christ.

Bonnke also convened a conference for 4000 native evangelists from all across Africa. This meeting served to spark personal revival in the hearts of those believers and to further spread the witness of the Gospel and Christian revival.

In strife-torn *South Africa*, revival is spreading like a prairie fire. Dr. Lawrence McCrystal says repentance is playing a key factor in South African revival. "We have done things that we are not proud of and have discriminated unfairly," he says, adding, "the people are repenting."

Evangelist Benny Hinn says, "I have never seen a revival like the one I'm seeing now." Despite the political and racial strife, revival *is* taking place, *right now*, in South Africa. The Great Commission is not being stopped by the tide of current events.

Great churches have sprung up all over the country--all multi-racial and eager to win souls and establish Christian schools. Hundreds of new churches have opened during the past decade under the leadership of Ray McCauley of Johannesburg. A one-time "Mr. South Africa" and "Mr. Universe" contender (in 1970), McCauley is pastor of the largest congregation in the nation. Rhema Bible Church in Johannesburg has some 8000 members.

Rev. Ed Reobert has pastored Hatfield Baptist Church in Pretoria for 25 years. The church has over 5000 members. Although from differing Christian backgrounds, Reobert and McCauley have led a movement of spiritual cooperation among Bible-believing congregations, demonstrating *love* to a nation (and world) obsessed with hate and strife--even among Western believers.

Hatred and discord are easy to stir up anywhere. Communists, working through the African National Congress, focus only on the problems of apartheid. The world's press concentrates on this single aspect of South African life. Because the media concentrates on the negative aspects of the nation's past and present, it is missing the greatest news event ever: Africa's--

FIRST GREAT AWAKENING.

Israel

In some respects, it would have been appropriate to start with a look at the nation of Israel as it relates to world evangelization. The good news of the Gospel was to be given "to the Jew first." Jesus said the Great Commission should be carried out so that evangelism was shared first in Israel before it was to go to the Gentiles.

Many of Jesus' parables centered around the

theme of the Jews' rejection of Jesus Christ. Israel, to be "scattered" and "regathered," was one of the major themes of the Old Testament prophecies. Israel established in the Palestinian homeland is likewise a fulfillment of many Old Testament prophecies.

All of these prophecies and principles, in relation to the Great Commission and Acts 1:8, indicate a chronology for the preaching of the Gospel: first to Israel, then to the Gentiles throughout the Church Age. The Gospel would have its greatest impact on the nation of Israel at the *end* of the Church Age, just before the Apocalypse.

In July 1987 I was invited to speak at a conference where I shared the platform with a converted Jew. During the meeting he mentioned that a number of Jews were being saved. After the meeting I asked him for more information. He wrote down my questions and later researched them and sent his answers to my office.

He reported to me that Rabbi Joseph Silivechi, a student of revelation and mystical religion, is a "rabbi to rabbis." Although Rabbi Silivechi is from New York, he travels to Israel on a monthly basis. This rabbi has proclaimed Jesus Christ as the Messiah.

Another Jewish scholar, Rabbi Pion, said to be the greatest Hebrew writer since Ezra, has written and published this statement: "It's time that we who know, accept Jesus Christ as the Messiah as an act of faith." Many, many thousands of Jews have already done so, as an act of faith, and have become fundamental, Bible-believing "completed" Jews.

Over 10,000 Jewish believers have been identified during the period of 1979 to 1987. The Messianic Jewish movement of the 1970's has resulted in over 146 "Messianic Synagogues," with the following provisions as part of their response of faith:

1. Repentance and turning to God.
2. Water baptism.
3. Acceptance of Jesus Christ as Savior
   and Lord.

Something significant is taking place through-out the world. As never before during the Church Age (since the days of the apostles), Jews are becoming followers of Jesus Christ in unprece-dented numbers. They are becoming organized and are themselves now involved in carrying out the Great Commission.

This First Awakening in many of the world's countries and the Third Great Awakening in the United States repre-sents a universal outpouring of God's Spirit, which is in fact now a--

WORLD AWAKENING.

Some will read of these awakenings and remark, "But these are not genuine; perhaps they represent the *Great Apostasy* found in the Book of the Revelation which will come on the world in the End Time."
Historically, there is a pattern of events:

1. God will do a great work.
2. It is overlooked by the world.
3. It is often rejected by many contemporaries.
4. As it peaks, it is imitated by the religious world with cultism and apostasy.
5. Then this movement is recognized by the world.

This World Awakening should be peaking between the early and mid-90's, and the apostate counter-movement should be flourishing by the late 90's. This will set the stage for the final apostasy, the Rapture of the true Church, and the appearance of the Antichrist. If you perceive this present

Awakening to be an apostasy, please note that it exalts Jesus Christ, proclaims God's Word, and features the Great Commission and world evangelization.

When it comes to apostasy, **STICK AROUND--**

"YOU AIN'T SEEN NUTHIN' YET."

10

A GREAT MULTITUDE

During 1986, in Africa and Asia alone, there was *an average of 1000 new churches opened every week!* There was an average of *78,000 new converts added daily* to all "Christian" denominations. In Latin America there are 65 new churches started every day. During the past two decades, Christianity has become the most *universal* and *extensive* religion in history.

In 1987, in the Baptist denomination alone, nearly a *million new members* were added to almost 130,000 local Baptist churches for a total of over 34 million members worldwide. This figure includes only baptized believers. Young children and new inquirers push the total of those in the world Baptist community to about 65 million.

When I was in college, Muslims, Hindus, Buddhists, Catholics, and Jews were the most difficult people to reach for Jesus Christ. Very few missionaries penetrated the religious exterior of these five groups and reached them with the Gospel in any considerable way. But God has declared, "And it shall come to pass in the last days . . . I will pour out of my

Spirit upon all flesh . . ." (Acts 2:17).

This outpouring spoken of in Acts 2:17 is now here. People are coming to Christ by the hundreds of thousands from all corners of the earth, and these conversions appear to be genuine. These people are building churches, starting Christian schools, sending forth missionaries, and taking the Gospel to the "uttermost parts of the earth."

The great "end-time" harvest of souls predicted in Biblical prophecies is taking place on a global scale at this very moment. We are living during the *greatest awakening* in all the days of the New Testament church. It is the most significant fulfillment of the Great Commission since Jesus gave the imperative to the Church just before His ascension. This "awakening" is no doubt the greatest spiritual phenomenon ever.

If such a great event is happening, why do the American people not know about it? After all, Americans are probably the best-informed people on earth.

I began this book with the statement, "The average Christian is as much in the dark as the world in general when it comes to seeing and understanding the *most significant facts, trends, and events.*

The mass media reflects a world-view that is secular, humanistic, and even anti-religious. That is why, as a *Christianity Today* article explains, the media is missing the *"greatest scoop"* of the century: "The failure to observe at all--not to mention to analyze and explain--the rise of evangelical Christianity in the U.S. (or around the world, for that matter) over two decades must constitute one of the greatest modern blind spots of the American journalistic mind" (*Christianity Today*, March 4, 1988).

Most of the secular media take an anti-religious bias and categorize Christians by such words as "fanatic fundamentalists" and "religious extremists." Yet they use no such "loaded" terms to describe the views of secular humanists, who always appear as more tolerant, understanding, and enlightened.

In a 1982 survey, 54 percent of the 240 journalists and broadcasters who responded classified themselves as being "left of the political center," and a majority said they were not religious. Many of their articles and features ridicule theistic values as archaic and outmoded. Many reporters and broadcast journalists are not just "overwhelmingly secular in their world-view, they tend not to respect religious faith in general, and, for the most part, they espouse a system of values inherently hostile to the traditional Western values handed down in the Bible . . . ." (*Christianity Today*, March 4, 1988, p. 12).

Following World War II, over 100 *new* nations were established and became a part of the United Nations. The media covered these events quite well.

Yet, in 1984, David Barrett reported in his *World Christian Encyclopedia* that, "There are today Christians and organized Christian churches in every inhabited country on earth." This news was ignored by the media.

The *Great Movement* of God in the 1600's was the immigration of Pilgrims and Puritans to the New World to establish a Christian government. In the 1700's a *Great Awakening* brought to fruition this dream of a Christian nation through independence, a Constitution, and a system of commerce and free enterprise. The newly formed United States of America reflected theistic values and brought about an Industrial Revolution to finance world evangelization.

The 1800's ushered in the *Second Great Awakening* and the beginning of the greatest expression of the fulfillment of the Great Commission on every continent. Population began to increase worldwide, and churches began to grow. Churches developed missionary programs, and the Gospel was sent around the world.

World War II and the following period of development laid the foundation for the *Third Great Awakening*, which really began to grow in significance and influence by the 1970's. Intercontinental travel, space-age communications, and unprecedented power played an important role in this Awakening, making it physically possible to "go into all the world," to "preach/teach . . . all people" (in their native tongue)--and to accomplish the entire task in a reasonable time frame.

During the Third Great Awakening, *two amazing phenomena* complemented each other in a significant demonstration of the power and intellect of God.

The *first phenomenon* was the unparalleled *international* impact of the Gospel along with the scope and intensity of the Holy Spirit's ministry. The *Third Great Awakening* was not just an American event--it had become a WORLD AWAKENING.

> "Greatest Awakening in all days of New Testament Church."

> "Greatest fulfillment of Great Commission."

> "Every inhabited country on earth . . ."

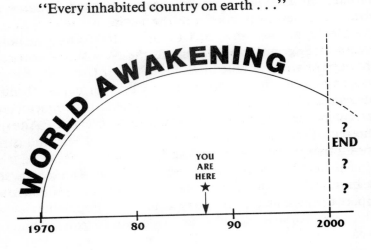

"The *GREATEST period* in the *HISTORY* of the *WORLD*"

Have you ever entered a shopping mall and stood by the mall directory or map with a marking and legend which said, "You are here"? That is almost how I sense our present relationship to history and eternity. We are living in the GREATEST PERIOD IN THE HISTORY OF THE WORLD: the most amazing period of the outpouring of God's Spirit that has ever been witnessed. Yet, most believers do not have any idea that it is happening!

This great outpouring exceeds anything that has happened in the history of the world. Not only that--it is the first time *in all of history* that such a phenomenon is all but *universal*.

Why is it happening almost universally? World War I made Communism a national power; World War II made Communism a world power. During the 25 years that followed World War II, the march and conquest of Communism was uncontested by its real enemy: the Gospel of Jesus Christ.

Communism is not an animal or mechanical monster. It is a system of thought, a political expression of HUMANISM that organizes man collectively around "the big lie" in defiance of God. It was first expressed in the Garden of Eden, "Ye shall be as gods," and later illustrated at the Tower of Babel. Communism is a political/philosophical rebirth of this same ideology sown into cultures of the world through well-meaning people who are without God and who are desperate to change the world.

Communism, the antithesis of Christianity, is Satan's masterpiece to bring together the unbelieving world in a form of imitation or counterfeit of the universal Church under the influence of the Holy Spirit. From 1945 to 1970, nation after nation came under the control of Communism (the chains of political slavery) and Rational HUMANISM. The answer to Communism, a "last days" enslaving phenomenon, is the Gospel of Jesus Christ that sets men free.

NOW NOTICE!

It is highly significant that each nation which is now experiencing AWAKENING has been under the threat or dominion of political Communism or its philosophical format HUMANISM. By the end of the 1960's HUMANISM had America academically, politically, and judicially on her knees. The Third Awakening has now turned major corners, and HUMANISM is now on the decline. Humanism does not work, and its advocates are losing their influence and are being replaced by evangelical and fundamental voices.

It is also significant that other countries that are experiencing Awakening have either been under the control of a Communist government for years or have been viciously terrorized by a growing military regime. For example, Russia and China, after a full generation or more under Communism (Russia for 70 years and China for 30 years) have experienced every disillusionment of "the big lie" and have found it to be "wanting." (The pendulum always swings back in God's timing.)

The influence of Communism is now abating. The people are hungry for reality, and the leaders with higher character are beginning to surface and experiment with liberty. As the door begins to open, the Light of the Gospel (unknown to the last generation) streams into the darkness with a blinding flash. Indonesia, under the threat of Communism, has turned to Christ. South Korea turned to Christ following the Korean War. The Philippines, now fearful of a Communist military coup, are turning to Christ. All the nations of West, Central, South, and East Africa are being terrorized by Communism and are turning to Christ.

Southeast Asia has been threatened by Communism and many are turning to Christ. In the next few years South Koreans will be carrying the Gospel into North Korea, and North Korean Communism will moderate.

The primary nations not yet ripe for harvest are the British Commonwealth nations, Europe, and the Mediterranean and Middle Eastern nations (chiefly the Arab nations that surround Israel). It appears that the very first fruits of AWAKENING are now appearing in the Commonwealth nations and in Europe. By 1990 the symptoms should be manifest. I do not expect the North African and Middle Eastern nations to experience awakening until after the Rapture and the Battle of Armageddon and until the two witnesses are sent out and the Great Multitude of Revelation 7:9 is on the scene. Most of these will come from Israel's present foes now at war with God and each other.

By 1990 I expect the Polish government to moderate, as well as the Eastern European nations who have been under Communism since World War II. As the World Awakening begins to penetrate Europe, the people will begin to cry out to God, and like Russia and China, the governments will moderate and people will become open to the Gospel.

This *Great Awakening* is happening *right now* in countries representing more than 80 percent of the world's population. For the first time in history, the percentage of people being won to Christ is growing faster than the population.

This brings us to the *second most amazing phenomenon:*

THE POPULATION EXPLOSION.

The Apostle John, in prophecy wrote, ". . . I beheld, and, lo, *a great multitude*, which no man could number, of all nations, and kindreds, and people, and tongues, stood before the throne, and before the Lamb . . . ." (Revelation 7:9)

A GREAT MULTITUDE

As a young believer in the late 50's, I had trouble visualizing this scene in Heaven. It seemed to me that only a small number of people turn to Jesus Christ. I had a growing perception that "few are saved." This "few" established unconscious limits in my thinking and theological conclusions.

At that time I tended to look for others whose ideas matched my presuppositions and dismissed others whose ideas did not equate with mine. Other believers may have this same difficulty in understanding what God is doing outside their normal sphere, and in understanding what the verse in Revelation is telling us: "A great multitude, which no man could number . . ."

Is there a contradiction? Jesus said, "Straight is the gate and narrow is the way that leadeth unto life, and *few* there be that find it." John said "a great multitude." From where does this "great multitude" come? You are no doubt part of the first generation of the Church Age to be able to see the SIGNIFICANCE of this event and understand the great phenomenon which John describes in Revelation 7:9.

On December 22, 1986, the Topeka *Capital-Journal* carried a front-page article which noted, "In the next 14 years,

---

137

the earth's population will grow by more than the total number of people who inhabited the planet in 1850." The paper also reported that the U.S. Census Bureau has projected that by the year 2000, the population will be some 6.2 *billion*. The world population has already *doubled* just since 1950, and will double again by A.D. 2000.

WORLD POPULATION

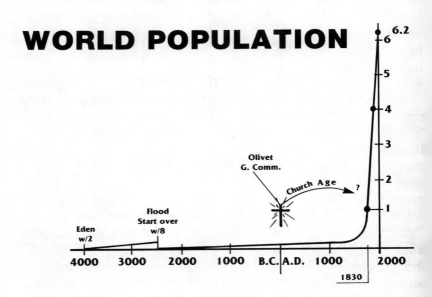

What is the *significance* of this second phenomenon? God started mankind with the creation of Adam and Eve in the Garden of Eden. Mankind multiplied until the time of the Great Flood; then God started over with Noah and seven of Noah's family. It is estimated that as few as 100 million people or as many as 300 million people lived from Noah's time to the time of Jesus. (While the *World Almanac* favors the 300 million figure, I lean toward the smaller number. For purposes of our illustration, it really does not matter.)

We know by modern fact-finding that the earth's population grew to *one billion* by 1830. From 1830 to 1975 the population grew to *four billion*, and (as mentioned already) will reach *6.2 billion* by A.D. 2000.

When I visited China in 1982, I saw public notices everywhere indicating that the Chinese were completing a census. This census revealed a Chinese population of 1.2 billion. China has been experiencing a population explosion just as is occurring everywhere else on the planet.

Population growth is inevitable. It is easily measured in contemporary history, relates factually to the accounts preserved in ancient history, and fits equally well and accurately to *Biblical* history and time frames. (The evolutionary hypothesis only contributes confusion and provides too many unanswerable questions about population growth: from what? from where? and for how long?)

It is sometimes difficult to understand statistics until they are put into some kind of perspective. During World War II the population of the Philippines was about eight million. Today, less than 50 years later, more than *60 million* people live in the Philippines. The majority of the Filipino race *who have ever lived* are living today. This illustrates the present world scene.

What is so amazing about the population growth is the "grand finale," which we are permitted to see and experience on an international scale *in our life*. For example, if we take the illustration regarding population growth in the Philippines and relate it to the entire world, we can perceive significant and amazing facts.

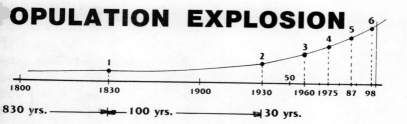

POPULATION EXPLOSION

If we use conservative Biblical dating methods, it took roughly six thousand years (or less) for the world's population to grow from two persons to *one billion* people. Then it took only one century (from 1830 to 1930) for the world's population to grow from one billion to *two billion*. That brings us to the years of the past generation. (My parents lived during this time, and I was born shortly thereafter.)

Then by 1960, in less than 30 years (*one-third of a century*), the population grew from two billion to *three billion*. Most of the present generation was alive at that time.

Then, it took *just 15 years* to add another billion (four billion by 1975), and *12 years later* the world population reached *five billion*. This significant event was marked on July 12, 1987. Eleven years after that date, the world population is expected to be *six billion*.

It is only now that we can see the effects of the two amazing "end-time" phenomena:

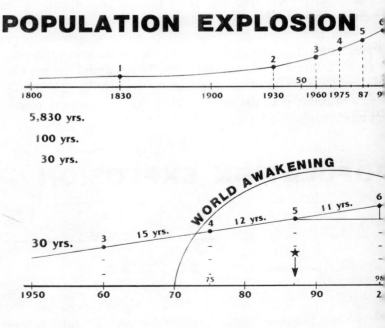

POPULATION EXPLOSION

5,830 yrs.

100 yrs.

30 yrs.

WORLD AWAKENING

30 yrs.

Jesus said "few," and John said "a great multitude." ow can both of these concepts be true? Here is one explana- n.

For about 6000 years, *"few" were saved.* But God has rposed to conduct an "end-time" harvest during the last neration of the Church Age. The last 50 years of this llennium in which we are now living represent about .8 per- t, which is less than one percent of historical time. During percent of recorded history (which is the RULE), *few* were ed. Then during the end-time harvest (the last one percent time), a "great multitude" will be saved. In any case, the eption does not nullify the rule, it establishes the rule.

The last great spiritual end-time harvest is occurring dur- God's predestined population explosion and Great Awak- ng. Jesus was born in "the fulness of time," when the old rld had established language, culture, travel, and mmunication--and a 200-year peace (Pax Romana). But w, as the world population explodes, travel, communica- n, and knowledge have likewise exploded, propelling man- d to a "zenith" of modern civilization at the end of this lennium.

It is in this context that we realize how much responsi- ty has been given to the Church of these "end-times." In nputing known facts into reasonable conclusions, some tling perceptions and assumptions stand out:

1. Most of the *people God created* are *alive!*
2. Most of the *people for whom Christ dies ARE ALIVE RIGHT NOW!*
3. Most of the *people for whom the Great Commission was given* are now *living!*
4. There are *more people alive* than have lived and died *before* now!

One night soon after New Year's in 1987, I went to bed these startling conclusions and perceptions fresh on my d. As quickly as I dozed off, I was roused from sleep with w thought. I promptly got out of bed and wrote down the ght which was burning in my mind and heart:

Most of the saints at the Marriage Supper of the Lamb will have lived and been saved during my lifetime and during this great--

WORLD AWAKENING!

The next day as I reflected over this great thought, wondered how many this great multitude might be. If the Church were caught up and taken to Heaven today, how many could be among that number? Then the statistics for the *World Awakening* began to come alive:

In	America	- 70 million
	China	- 50 million
	Russia	- 40 million
	Korea	- 10 million
	Indonesia	- 20 million
	India	- 20 million
	Africa	- 150 million
	Latin America	- 20 million
	Europe	- 10 million
	In other countries	- 10 million

I estimated that the total would come to some *400 million*. Then I added another 100 million babies who have been murdered by abortions--some 20 million just in America alone since 1970, plus those from Russia, China, and other countries--bringing the total to half a billion for today's era.

Add in the number of babies and youngsters who die when child and infant mortality was great (until this century

en, add the number of all the saints of Old Testament
nes and the believers from the Church Age--from the time
the apostles up to this age yet uncounted. Then add the rest
be saved the last decade of this century when the numbers
exploding, plus the "great multitude" of Revelation 7:9
it will come out of the Great Tribulation.

When those who died in the past are added to the 500
llion of modern era saints, it pushes my guess to *one billion*
nts at the Marriage Supper of the Lamb!

Can you picture one billion people?

Think about the biggest crowd you can imagine--perhaps
unprecedented 100,000 people in a giant stadium to watch
Rose Bowl game. Now picture *nine more* stadium crowds
same size. When all of these are put together, that is only
million people.

Now, if it is possible in your imagination, multiply by ten
se ten football stadiums that are packed with people. If
can picture the results, it is still only *ten million*. So you
e to multiply that again by ten to get 100 million; then you
e to multiply that result by ten to get a billion.

A billion people is *10,000 football stadium crowds of
,000!* Now imagine that host of voices singing praise to
d and the Lamb! I am not sure what size table will be at the
rriage Supper of the Lamb, but be assured it will take a
at number of angels (and a lot of dishes and silverware) to
e a billion saints.

Does one billion believers sound reasonable?

In light of the *total* population from the time of Adam to
. 2000, my own computed guess comes to about 10 billion
ple who have lived, are living, or will be born by the year
.

In reflecting on God's plan and purpose "from the foun-
ons of the earth" through the fall of man; through the
nises of the prophets; through the incarnation, tempta-
s, and atonement of Jesus Christ; through the Church
; and to the Second Coming--is it too much to expect God
eceive (through His redemption and restoration) a *tithe* of
n humanity to populate the New Jerusalem.

It does not sound unreasonable to expect ten percent to

worship God for all eternity. Imagine the compounded joy o
one billion saints worshiping, singing, and praising Go
because He redeemed them. Jesus did not die for just
handful--to love, worship, and praise Him for all eternity
The Revelation speaks of a conquering, victorious GREAT
MULTITUDE!

Amazingly, in eternity a believer from this great multi
tude will not be "lost in the crowd." Although there might b
a billion souls before the throne, it will not in any way lim
access to Him. In fact, access to God will have an infinitel
enhanced reality and significance--far more real and preciou
than the time you spend alone with God now.

He knows each of us by the new name He has given th
redeemed. He will call us by that name, and we will stan
before Him sinless and righteous--to LOVE and SERVE HIM
perpetually, and we will call Him LORD.

> *After this I beheld, and, lo, a great multitude,*
> *which no man could number, of all nations, and*
> *kindreds, and people, and tongues, stood before*
> *the throne, and before the Lamb, clothed with*
> *white robes, and palms in their hands.*
>
> *--Revelation 7:9*

11

"THE END":
??? A.D. 2000 ???

In the Olivet Discourse and in His Great Commission, Jesus spoke of *"the END."* He also said, ". . . for ye know neither the *day* nor the *hour* wherein the Son of man cometh" (Matthew 25:13).

However, before He gave this caution, Jesus gave signs (or clues) so a person who is "watching" will have evidence to know the time is imminent. He said, "Watch therefore: ..." (Matthew 24:42) and ". . . When these things begin to come to pass, then look up . . . your redemption draweth nigh" (Luke 21:28). He gave this caution to all of the Church, most of whom are alive and able to be watching NOW. In Luke 21:31 Jesus repeats the idea with only a slight vocabulary change: ". . . when ye see *these things* come to pass, know ye that the *kingdom of God* is *nigh at hand.*" He gave us, the Church today, this admonition.

In Matthew 24:3 the disciples expressed interest in knowing about the *end* of the *world.* Following their inquiry, Jesus begins His answer in a clear and meaningful way, in what apparently must refer to *"the end."* From verse 4 through verse

13 of Matthew 24, Jesus speaks only of the *end of the age.*

This passage of Scripture is related to several other key verses having the same significance and relating directly to the Great Commission and to the *signs* of the *end*:

"Go ye into all the world . . ." (Mark 16:15).

"Go ye therefore, and teach all nations . . ." (Matthew 28:19).

". . . Repentance and remission of sins should be preached in his name among all nations . . ." (Luke 24:47).

". . . the gospel must first be published among all nations . . ." (Mark 13:10).

". . . this gospel shall be preached in the whole world . . ." (Matthew 26:13).

For centuries, Jesus' commission sounded like a dream that could never come true. But we have *seen* its fulfillment *in our lifetimes.* David Barrett says in his *World Christian Encyclopedia* that Christianity has been preached in every inhabited country of the earth and there are now churches in every nation on earth.

Today it is possible to declare what could not have been said before 1970:

THE GREAT COMMISSION HAS BEEN FULFILLED!

If there is still any question regarding the Great Commission having been fulfilled, it would probably relate to *how much preaching* and *teaching* are required for its *complete* fulfillment. The Bible does not require that all hear a prophet or that all respond in order for the Great Commission to be fulfilled.

In the companion passage in Luke 21 where Jesus discusses His return, He says, "This generation shall not pass away, till all be fulfilled" (Luke 21:32). Some scholars believe that the term *generation* means *race* and that Jesus was referring to Israel--which would "not pass away." In fact, Israel became an independent nation May 14, 1948, after nearly 2000 years of being scattered across the earth.

In *1997*, Israel will observe her forty-ninth birthday in the land with a great sabbatical year of jubilee. This observance could likewise be a very significant event.

Nevertheless, the *most significant* thing is what Jesus said in relation to the *end*, which proves to my satisfaction that He will return before this present generation passes from the scene, probably by A.D. 2000.

Jesus made a most significant statement in Matthew 24:14 (right after He had given the signs of His return in verses four through eight) when He gave one condition that was necessary for His coming--that
". . . this gospel of the kingdom shall be preached in all the world for a witness unto all nations; and--

THEN SHALL THE END COME."

Has this happened? Has the Gospel been preached in all the world? To all nations?

The condition does not require the preaching of the Gospel to every individual of every country in order to be complete. Men know intuitively of the truth. The obligation from God's Word is not to reach each individual, but for ". . . this gospel of the kingdom" to be ". . . preached *in all the world* for a *witness unto all nations* . . ." The greatest truths of the Bible are also written in the hearts of all people. Missionary Don Richardson's book *Eternity in Their Hearts* is a great polemic in print to illustrate this principle that the conscience of man bears witness to God's existence.

Many Christian organizations are looking at the time between now and the end of this century to complete the fulfillment of Jesus' words and His Great Commission. A number of Christian groups, denominations, and individuals have set the year 2000 as the climax of serious, intense evangelistic efforts.

By the year 1987, ninety-seven percent of the people of the world had God's Word in their own language. Can the task be completed for the remaining three percent by A.D. 2000?

The Lausanne Committee for World Evangelization, organized by the Billy Graham Evangelistic Association, is focusing on fulfilled global evangelization by *the year 2000*.

Southern Baptists are organized to spread the Gospel to all people by *the year 2000*. *Bold Missions Thrust* is a strategy for global evangelism by the Southern Baptist denomination. It emphasizes discipleship and brings together scores of denominational agencies, thousands of churches, and millions of Christians. It is a highly organized missions thrust designed to plant churches around the world.

The *North American Congress on the Holy Spirit and World Evangelization* was attended by nearly 50,000 members of 40 denominations, ministries, and fellowships. The focus of the event was to learn how to cooperatively preach the Gospel to all nations by *the year 2000*.

New Life 2000, spearheaded by Dr. Bill Bright of *Campus Crusade for Christ*, is an ambitious plan to train *hundreds of millions* and bring the Gospel to the world's people by the end of the century. Billy Graham is honorary chairman. Bill Bright expects that *one billion* people will be converted to the Christian faith through New Life 2000 efforts. The goal is continuation, expansion, and acceleration of evangelistic and missionary activities.

Dr. Bright's Campus Crusade organization is also planning *Explo* conferences to help accelerate the fulfillment of the Great Commission. Campus Crusade's *Here's Life* program, designed for city-wide campaigns, will be used extensively. In villages where such sophisticated efforts will not work, Campus Crusade will use radio and films.

According to Campus Crusade, over *400 million* people in 110 countries have viewed the film *Jesus*, which is based very closely on the Gospel of Luke and consists mainly of Scripture. The film has been released in 110 languages, with a goal of translating it into 271 major languages and dialects.

Millions have viewed the film *Jesus* and have made decisions to accept Jesus Christ as Lord and Savior. It was shown in London and drew more viewers than *Mr. T.* It was also shown by nationals in every Catholic church in Poland.

It is also being shown in small villages around the world. For example, Pastor David Winston, who had bought a copy of *Jesus* in Spanish for $1100, works in Mexico each summer. He recently took the film with him to Acapulco but did not take a projector. He wanted to show the film but could not locate a projector there.

While Pastor Winston was visiting in a village, the director of an orphanage mentioned that he had an antique Bell and Howell projector that had just been returned that morning from Mexico City where it had been repaired (it had been gone for a year). Pastor Winston took this projector, set it up on a street corner, used the side of a house for a screen, and showed the film *Jesus*. One hundred people watched the film and 25 received Christ as Savior.

David Wilkerson's life story, made into the film *The Cross and the Switchblade*, has been used for witnessing in more than 65 countries. It has appealed to large urban audiences around the world.

Billy Graham was the first to see the value of films in evangelism. His *World Wide Pictures* produced *The Hiding Place* (based on the life of Corrie Ten Boom) and *Joni* (the story of Joni Erickson-Tada).

During these latter days of the twentieth century, film and video programs are having an impact for Christ around the world. In America, however, films are not nearly as effective because of the vast number of films that are available to Americans.

Overseas film evangelists often hang a sheet in the middle of a town square at sunset and use the sheet as a screen on which to project a film. People will sit on both sides of the makeshift screen, watching intently. This is the first time for many of them to ever see a film and to hear the Gospel in their own language.

The Christian motion picture has become a powerful overseas evangelistic tool for these latter days of the twentieth century. However, it is not the only tool.

Three major Christian broadcasting organizations are cooperating in a joint goal to bring the Gospel to the entire world by radio. Pioneer missionary radio station *HCJB, Far East Broadcasting Company*, and *Trans World Radio* plan to use short-wave radio technology to encircle the planet earth with Gospel radio signals. The U.S.-based *CBN* television network has similar plans for Christian television.

CBN's *Operation Blessing* was started as a *relief service* outreach of the organization. They have since provided food, shelter, and clothing for victims of disasters such as earthquakes, floods, famines, and other terrible events. *World Vision* and *Medical Assistance Programs* are two other major evangelical agencies which have raised millions of dollars for similar needs, such as for the victims of the African famines.

The *U.S. Center for World Missions* plans to challenge mission groups to reach 17,000 "unreached people groups" and hasten worldwide evangelism by the year 2000. All the member nations of the United Nations now have churches that are sending out missionaries. However, the mission agencies of the world have located small scattered families and tribes who have yet to hear the Gospel.

Bibles For The World, based in Wheaton, Illinois, is headed by Dr. Rochunga Pudaite, a native of India. The organization has launched *"Target 2000,"* which is described as "a new strategy to reach our entire world with the Word of God by the end of the twentieth century." Their plan is to use the world's telephone directories as a mailing list and mail one billion Bibles by A.D. 2000.

Dr. Pudaite has tested the idea in over 60 countries, having already mailed over nine million New Testaments in 18 languages. Responses to the mailings pour into the Wheaton office daily, a great number of them telling of their conversion to Jesus Christ.

Nearly 98 percent of the world has God's Word, or a portion of it, in their own native tongue. The problem is no longer translation, but distribution.

Bibles For The World believes that its task will help reach the world with God's Word and will also hasten the fulfillment of Biblical prophecy: "And this gospel of the kingdom shall be preached in all the world for a witness unto all nations; and then shall the end come" (Matthew 24:14).

Their vision is for the Church to finish the unfinished task of publishing the Bible among all nations through the co-operative efforts of 100,000 churches and a million individual Christians. "We appeal to all pastors and local church leaders to enlist just ten families from each congregation who will commit themselves to mail at least 12 Bibles each month," Dr. Pudaite explains. "Each volunteer is asked to pay the postage to mail the Bibles and to pray for each person who will receive one."

Bibles For The World supplies the New Testaments at no cost to those who help. They are shipped in "12-paks"--12 Bibles or New Testaments, 12 self-sealing wrappers, and 12 pre-addressed labels. The organization is seeking a capital fund of $20 million to print 12 million Bible 12-paks as a launching project of the plan.

Dr. Pudaite says, "Our test results have convinced us that:

1. The people of the world want to know who Jesus really is;
2. The Bible is the authoritative book about Jesus Christ and His plan of salvation for all mankind;
3. 'The Word of God is quick and powerful' and is perfectly capable to produce fruit for the king-dom; and
4. The Church of Jesus Christ must work together to let the whole world read God's Word."

Evangelists Luis Palau, Billy Graham, Jimmy Swaggart, and others have held crusades both over-seas and in America. During the 1980's, Dr. Gra-ham has even held crusades in Communist nations.

The Billy Graham Evangelistic Association has been an organizing force behind the evangelism conventions in Lausanne (1974) and Amsterdam (1986), which brought together thousands of dynamic, committed evangelists and church workers from around the world.

A planned *Congress on Evangelism* in Lausanne (1989) will make workshops and strategies available to *millions* of believers around the world who cannot attend in person but who can take part through the *International Satellite Mission* of the BGEA. Technology will be used that only a few years ago was science fiction. Television signals via satellite, global teleconferencing, and instantaneous communications were only dreams 25 years ago. Today they are tools to use to change the world by the end of this millennium.

David Barrett, author of *World Christian Encyclopedia*, comments on the tremendous revival and evangelistic efforts of these "last days," saying that there have been perhaps some 300 "master plans" for world evangelization and most have failed.

Most of these plans failed because they were conceived in isolation. There was no means of coordinating them. Today, with computers and satellites, leaders and partners can be brought closer together to work out a role for all participants to be effective worldwide. Christians are catalysts and can "network" ideas, resources, and personnel to get the job done.

It is precisely in this area of technical and managerial expertise that Americans can be used best--as support teams and not so much as the "front line" troops. Since English is the international language of commerce and economics, Western missionaries who are sent as technicians and advisors will generally be effective.

Youth With a Mission (YWAM) targets other nations for evangelism and uses American missionaries for strategy and approach ideas. (YWAM was started by Loren Cunningham in 1960 as an interdenominational youth ministry.) Some 100,000 YWAM workers have visited 200 countries to share their faith with millions.

Traditional Western missionary organizations are beginning to see their role as one of *assisting* in global evangelism and are not presuming to initiate and control what is happening overseas. *Wycliffe Bible Translators International* trains mostly U.S. citizens and other Westerners for its specialty. The agency has grown significantly since 1970, and one of its goals is to give the Bible or portions of Scripture to the estimated 3000 language groups which still do not have God's Word in their own native tongues. Another of Wycliffe's goals is to recruit another 5000 workers to be involved in the translation ministry, to bring God's Word to the three percent of the world which still have no Bible in their own tongues.

Just a generation ago, it took a lifetime for a translator to decipher a language and translate the Bible. Today much of that work can be done efficiently by computer, therefore, linguists expect that the goal of 100 percent translation by *the year 2000* is a reasonable one.

Missionary experts have also identified from 16,000 to 17,000 "hidden peoples"--small tribal groups and families which are isolated and have not yet heard the Gospel. These mission agencies feel that the goal of taking the Gospel to this remainder of unreached people can be achieved through modern technological assistance by the year 2000.

If the Great Commission has not yet been fulfilled completely, it should be by A.D. 2000. *"And then shall the end come."*

12

WORLD CONDITIONS: 2000

Do you remember the little guy who painted himself into a corner? Humanity has been doing the same thing in a number of ways this century. The day is long gone when men or tribes could just pack up and leave their problems behind. In today's world, mankind has catastrophic conditions to deal with: an exploding population, a shrinking globe, a declining world economy, and a diminishing land area with no new real estate on God's drawing board - to name only a few. We have inadvertently created all these problems, and we are unable to solve them. Mankind is painting himself into a corner from which there is no way out.

1. GLOBAL ECOLOGY

The first corner that man is painting himself into is the crisis of ecology. Global ecology is all but doomed. We are releasing into the atmosphere chemicals that not only pollute our air and environment but also cause diseases and other concerns.

Ironically, man has created pesticides and fertilizers to

improve agriculture, but these same products have wiped out enormous numbers of fish, plants, and animals. Now the balance of nature is threatened. DDT alone has destroyed entire generations of fish, birds, and other wildlife.

True, authorities have banned DDT and are careful about using other chemicals. But disasters still abound, as evidenced by the harmful after-effects of the use of "agent orange" in Viet Nam and the terrible accident in Phopal, India where thousands died as a result of a chemical leak. The U.S. and Russia have stockpiled enough nerve gases to wipe out entire nations.

Other chemicals in the atmosphere are depleting the ozone layer. On August 7, 1988, "A.B.C. News" reported that Soviet leaders are shocked at reduced ozone layers over major cities, including Moscow. They believe this condition causes milder winters and hotter summers. One scientist says, "Man is irreversibly altering the ability of our atmosphere to support life."

Without enough ozone, solar radiation will wreak deadly havoc. Already, medical authorities report a growing surge in the number of skin cancers, diseases, and other problems caused by excessive ultra-violet radiation. Not only that but also the air we breathe is killing us. Smog in big cities is thick enough to change the blue sky to yellow and brown. Airplanes, trains, cars, and trucks spew forth thousands of tons of pollutants.

Are the plagues of Revelation 15 and 16 becoming reality in our generation? Since the middle of the 18th century, the industrialized countries have released 200 billion tons of carbon dioxide into the atmosphere. This amount will increase by A.D. 2000 to over *400 million tons* of air pollutants *annually*. Scientists worry about our planet's facing another "greenhouse" effect or undergoing disastrous climatic changes, such as the melting of polar ice or similar climatic catastrophes.

Last year the U.S. Navy reported that an iceberg nearly 100 miles long had broken free from the Antarctic ice shelf. In 1986, two other huge icebergs broke away. In the last century the sea levels have risen half a foot. A major polar ice melt would be disastrous. A rise of just two feet in sea levels would flood most major port cities of the world.

As the sun's rays are held back, scientists predict an average global warming of from one to two degrees by A.D. 2000 and from two to four degrees by A.D. 2020. That small rise in the earth's average temperature is apparently enough to melt even more Arctic and Antarctic polar ice and further raise the level of the oceans. As a result, many of the world's coastal cities may well sink completely under water; lowlands and beaches could be flooded and destroyed soon after the turn of the century.

The geography of much of the world will be changed drastically - perhaps at great loss of life.

This glut of carbon dioxide is also caused in part by another man-created problem: deforestation.

Every year more and more millions of acres of forest and jungle are killed through "acid rain," while millions more are bulldozed to make room for "civilization." Acid rain has killed plankton in the lakes and seas which create much of the world's oxygen. Although forests make up less than 10% of the planet's area, they produce the rest of the world's oxygen supply.

Every year the planet loses hundreds of square miles of rain forest and agricultural land to deserts. The famous "Dust Bowl" in the central U.S. is a typical example of how quickly civilization, unchecked, can destroy a land. The huge Arabian Desert in Egypt, between the Red Sea and the Nile River, is 70 thousand square miles of desert. Each year, the desert extends by hundreds of acres per day into Sudan, Libya, Chad, and other bordering countries.

The time may occur sooner than we think when ozone depletion, air pollution, carbon dioxide in the atmosphere, or depletion of oxygen sources (or all of these!) will create a planetary crisis capable of destroying all life.

2. OVERPOPULATION

A parallel problem is the "population bomb."
At the time of Jesus' birth, a maximum of 250 million

people were living. It took over 1,500 years for that number to double, but only 300 years for it to double again. Today four babies are born every second, while two people die every second - a net gain of two persons every second.

If the present population growth rate continues unchecked, there will be over *20 billion people* on earth in just 100 years.

We need not wait for a crisis caused by overpopulation. It already exists. Up to 70% of the world's population is in third world countries, in nations least prepared or least capable of dealing with the problems of overpopulation.

A recent means of "dealing" with the problem of overpopulation is the course of natural disaster. Famines have recently claimed *millions of lives* in Africa, Asia, and other areas of the world. The problems of food supply and political turmoil increase with population growth. Earthquakes and volcanic eruptions in Iran, Colombia, Mexico, Turkey, China, and other countries have also taken millions of lives - almost in direct response to the prophecies of Matthew 25 (which we will examine later in this chapter).

Every one of the world's ecological problems is compounded by overpopulation. Even in the "first world" countries, governments are trying to cope with housing, transportation, food, and agricultural problems made more acute by ecological abuses and overpopulation. Scientists say "D-Day" for the population crisis is at or near A.D. 2000.

There is no question but that mankind is painting itself into another corner - overpopulation.

3. NUCLEAR DESTRUCTION

As if these problems were not enough, there is yet another corner into which mankind has painted itself. On July 16, 1945, Robert Oppenheimer and Enrico Fermi awaited the tests of a new weapon on the bombing range of Alamogordo, New Mexico. The plutonium test bomb exploded atop a tower and made pre-dawn brighter than noonday. It generated a fireball with a temperature four times hotter than the sun's core. The blast had the force and shock-wave effect of some 10,000 *tons* of TNT.

President Harry Truman was advised to use the atomic bomb on Japan to end World War II. For the final defense of Japan, the Japanese war lords were planning to use some 10,000 *kamikaze* (suicide) planes, nearly 2.5 million troops, and over 30 million civil employees and militiamen, fighting hand-to-hand with spears, bows and arrows, or swords.

The casualties were expected to be *10 - 20 million Japanese* and at least *one million of the American or Allied forces*.

President Truman weighed this possibility of enormous carnage with the possibility of using the new A-bomb to *end* the war, avoiding an invasion conflict altogether.

On August 3rd, American planes flew over Hiroshima and dropped over 700 thousand leaflets warning the people to flee because the city would be destroyed in two days.

Two days later, the first nuclear bomb used in warfare exploded over the city. Of nearly 250 thousand people still in the city, 100,000 died on the spot from the effects.

Eleven days later, World War II ended with the surrender of Japan. An invasion was averted, saving literally millions of lives.

Historians tell us that it is only by God's grace and Hitler's madness that Germany did not get the atom bomb first.

A German-Jewish scientist was one of the first to perfect the atomic theory in the late 1930's and early 1940's. Because he was a Jew, Hitler refused to see him, so the scientist fled Germany and helped America build the first atomic bomb.

It is horrible to even contemplate what the world would be like if Hitler had been the first to use nuclear warfare in World War II.

Today, mankind is itself poised under the Damocles sword of nuclear annihilation. Tens of thousands of nuclear warheads are aimed at all the major cities of the world. *Each one* contains more destruction than a *hundred* Hiroshimas.

For years the two super powers have exercised remarkable restraint. It's only by God's grace that we have not blown up the world, in anger or even by accident.

Yet, even if the two major powers - America and the

Soviet Union - were to eliminate all nuclear weapons, there would still be a danger.

Last year Brazil became the tenth country to develop the technology to make a nuclear bomb. Others include England, France, West Germany, the Netherlands, Japan, China, and Argentina. Some other countries are also rumored to now have the bomb: Israel, India, Pakistan, and South Africa.

Next year, perhaps others will have the capability. What will happen between India and Pakistan if one or both develop a nuclear bomb? What if Idi Amin or Pol Pot had used atomic weapons in their mass murders? Their already shameful killings would be unthinkably magnified in scope.

Or, what if Libya's Muammar el-Qaddafi get his hands on a bomb and decides to use it? Or the Ayatollah? The P.L.O. or I.R.A.? The question no longer is "Can such a thing happen?" but "When?" Even if a nuclear bomb is not set off, scientists say that disaster might come through another (worse) Chernobyl or Three-Mile Island accident - but with global implications.

There is a sense that maniacs are in control in some countries of the world. Terrorists often act irrationally and even strike out toward innocent parties. Bombs, grenades, and machine guns have massacred tourists and innocent bystanders in a Rome airport, an Irish church, an Arab mosque, and an Israeli school. Also, an elderly man in a wheelchair was gunned down and tossed overboard when terrorists captured a cruise ship. There is no safety anywhere from terrorists, and a terrorist with a nuclear bomb is the ultimate horror.

If America is "the most civilized Christian nation in the world," and yet we used the bomb at Nagasaki - unnecessarily, many believe - do you think Arafat, Qaddafi, or Khomeini would hesitate to use it, too?

Mankind has painted itself into a corner of nuclear destruction, and it is only a matter of time before the holocaust. There is no way out.

4. ARMAGEDDON

There is yet another corner into which mankind is painting itself. The Bible tells us that life will end at the very place where it began.

Armageddon used to be a word used in literature as a science fiction scenario. After all, how could armies of *millions* come together in one spot, and what would attract them?

Modern history shows us the stage is already set for the world's final destructive battle.

For 4,000 years "Isaac" and "Ishmael" have fought. The conflict has grown from two people, two families, and two tribes to a *host* of nations which dominate the Eastern world. Israel and the Arabs, Asia and Africa - along with Europe and America - have been drawn into the conflict.

Notice how some of the key players are already involved in the Mideast tensions: Yasser Arafat, Muammar el-Qaddafi, the Ayatollah Khomeini, King Hussein, Hosni Mubarak, Assad, and others.

As soon as the Eight-Year War between Iraq and Iran is settled and a brief period of peace ensues, the Arab world will again begin battling their sabres against Israel. For the last forty years the tension has been mounting and will, no doubt, be raised to its highest crescendo over the demands of the Palestinians. This could be the coming climax in view of the fact that the world consensus, for the last year, has been turning heavily against Israel because of the intensification of hostilities - and now the "Declaration of Independence" - within the borders of the land God promised to Abraham and his seed.

5. MORAL SUICIDE

Western culture took prayer out of the schools and brought sex education into the schools. The HUMANIST REVOLUTION gave the kids a green light on sexual expression, and the rest is history. It became culturally acceptable to sell contraceptives to youths and to give them away in school-based "health" clinics. Now it is culturally acceptable to use kids to advertise them in national magazines.

The constant promotion and practice of sexual liberation

has brought on the PLAGUE of AIDS. The experts recommend medical and mechanical solutions for a moral crisis. Mankind has painted itself into a corner of moral suicide.

CCN News (3/24/88) reported on the education of elementary school children regarding AIDS. A teacher was shown telling seven-year-old boys and girls how to use a condom, informing them that "condoms and clean needles protect them from AIDS."

The children are taught that sex and drugs are not the problems - but "safe sex" and "safe drugs" through mechanical, medical means will cope with AIDS.

By 1991, the total number of Americans *under thirteen* with AIDS infection will be 10 - 20 thousand.

The hard questions are already being asked: "Who will care for them?" and "What about children with AIDS and schools?"

April, 1987, Dr. Jonathan Mann, Director of the AIDS program for W.H.O. (World Health Organization) reported that AIDS cases have been reported in over 100 countries and is now an epidemic.

This deadly plague is expected to claim the lives of 100 million people before it runs its course! That's more than the total population of Britain and France.

That staggering statistic, according to one source, means more deaths from AIDS in a single decade than the combined fatalities of all the wars, atrocities, massacres, and plagues of the entire twentieth century (excluding China). The coming AIDS crisis will reach its peak by A.D. 2000.

Why does it seem that mankind has painted itself into a corner from so many different directions?

--Economists warn of a global market crash - expected before A.D. 2000 - that will cripple world economics . . .

--The AIDS crisis will peak with 100 million deaths by A.D. 2000 . . .

--The overpopulation crisis will peak with six billion people living on earth by A.D. 2000 . . .

--Experts predict that several terrorist nations will
have their own nuclear bombs by A.D. 2000 . . .

--Nearly 400 million tons of pollutants are dumped
every year into the air we breathe and may create
disastrous atmospheric conditions by A.D. 2000. . .

--Chemicals have depleted the ozone layer and
could cause a deadly outbreak of skin cancers by
A.D. 2000 . . .

--Scientists say a global warming effect may wipe
out major coastal cities by A.D. 2000 . . .

--Deforestation may seriously deplete our oxygen
levels by A.D. 2000 . . .

--Global climate changes may cause the worst
floods, droughts, and famines ever by A.D.
2000 . . .

--Peace within the Arab world could bring a unified
hostility against Israel in a climactic military campaign by A.D. 2000 . . .

Experts say humanity could cause its own extinction -
perhaps before this century ends. Is it merely coincidence that
they are saying the world might end by A.D. 2000?

Armageddon is a "code" word to signal the end. Jesus
gave other "clues" as to the characteristics, signs, and events
of these apocalyptic "perilous times" or "last days" (see
Matthew 24):

Matthew 24:6-15; 29-30; 50-51

"And ye shall hear of wars and rumours of
wars: see that ye be not troubled: for all these

things must come to pass, but the end is not yet. (v.6)

"For nation shall rise against nation, and kingdom against kingdom: and there shall be famines, and pestilences, and earthquakes, in divers places. (v.7)

"Then shall they deliver you up to be afflicted, and shall kill you: and ye shall be hated of all nations for my name's sake. (v.9)

"And many false prophets shall rise, and shall deceive many. (v.11)

"And because iniquity shall abound, the love of many shall wax cold. (v.12)

"And this gospel of the kingdom shall be preached in all the world for a witness unto all nations; and *then* shall *the end come*. (v.14)

"Immediately after the tribulation of those days shall the sun be darkened, and the moon shall not give her light, and the stars shall fall from heaven, and the powers of the heavens shall be shaken; (v.29)

"And then shall appear the sign of the Son of man in heaven; and then shall all the tribes of the earth mourn, and they shall see the Son of man coming in the clouds of heaven with power and great glory. (v.30)

"The lord of that servant shall come in a day when he looketh not for him, and in an hour that he is not aware of, (v.50)

"And shall cut him asunder, and appoint him his portion with the hypocrites: there shall be weeping and gnashing of teeth." (v.51)

JESUS SAID . . .

--*Wars and conflicts* will break out. (v.6)
--*Famines* will cause many deaths. (v.7)
--*Plagues* will also kill many more. (v.7)
--*Earthquakes* will happen in a number of locations. (v.7)

--*Sorrow* will be felt for the nation of Israel. (v.8)

--*Persecution* of Jews and *martyrdom* will take place. (v.9)

--*False prophets* (antichrists) will deceive many. (v.11)

--*Rampant sin* will characterize the times. (v.12) This is the KEY passage to identify the period of His coming:

--*"Great Tribulation"* will occur. (v.29)

--*Ecological and natural disasters* will take place. (v.29)

--The *Lord returns* in judgment. (v.30,50,51)

A similar list of events appears in Revelation 18:

Revelation 18:6-8; 11; 15; 19-21

"Reward her even as she rewarded you, and double unto her double according to her works; in the cup which she hath filled fill to her double. (v.6)

"How much she hath glorified herself, and lived deliciously, so much torment and sorrow give her; for she saith in her heart, I sit a queen, and am no widow, and shall see no sorrow. (v.7)

"Therefore shall her plagues come in one day, death, and mourning, and famine; and she shall be utterly burned with fire; for strong is the Lord God who judgeth her. (v.8)

"And the merchants of the earth shall weep and mourn over her; for no man buyeth their merchandise any more; (v.11)

"The merchants of these things, which were made rich by her, shall stand afar off for the fear of her torment, weeping and wailing, (v.15)

"And they cast dust on their heads, and cried, weeping and wailing, saying, Alas, alas, that great city, wherein were made rich all that had ships in the sea by reason of her costliness! for in one hour is she made desolate. (v.19)

"Rejoice over her, thou heaven, and ye holy apostles and prophets; for God hath avenged you on her. (v.20)

"And a mighty angel took up a stone like a great millstone, and cast it into the sea, saying, Thus with violence shall that great city Babylon be thrown down, and shall be found no more at all." (v.21)

--*Judgment and destruction* are coming. (v.6-8)

--*Famine* is predicted. (v.8)

--*Plagues* will bring death and mourning. (v.8)

--*Fiery destruction* will come. (v.8)

--There will be widespread *economic chaos*. (v.11, 15, 19)

--*Earthquakes, tidal waves, or volcanic eruptions.* (v.21)

Paul, in writing to Timothy, gave similar warnings:

II Timothy 3:1-6, 13

"This know also, that in the last days perilous times shall come. (v.1)

"For men shall be lovers of their own selves, covetous, boasters, proud, blasphemers, disobedient to parents, unthankful, unholy, (v.2)

"Without natural affection, trucebreakers, false accusers, incontinent, fierce, despisers of those that are good. (v.3)

"Traitors, heady, highminded, lovers of pleasures more than lovers of God; (v.4)

"Having a form of godliness, but denying the power thereof; from such turn away. (v.5)

"For of this sort are they which creep into houses, and lead captive silly women laden with sins, led away with divers lusts, (v.6)

"Ever learning, and never able to come to the knowledge of the truth. (v.7)

"But evil men and seducers shall wax worse

and worse, deceiving, and being deceived." (v.13)

--*Perilous times* will come. (v.1)

--People will be *utterly self-centered*. (v.2)

--They will be *greedy for money*. (v.2)

--Society will consist of *proud boasters*. (v.2)

--*Blasphemy* will be a natural characteristic. (v.2)

--Youth will be *disobedient, thankless, irreligious*. (v.2)

--People will be *unloving, unforgiving slanderers*. (v.3)

--They will be *savage and brutal* (violent). (v.3)

--*Hostility to all that is good* is part of their lifestyle. (v.3)

--These people will *lack sexual self-control*. (v.3)

--They will *betray their friends*. (v.4)

--And like hot-heads, they will *act without thought*, as people who put *sensual, immoral pleasure* and *vain amusements* ahead of worshipping God. (v.4)

--They will *invade homes* and *prey on women*. (v.6)

--They will be swayed by all kinds of *unnatural lusts and evil impulses*. (v.6)

--They have access to massive education resources but are blinded by the HUMANIST REVOLUTION and caught up in the deception of the New Age Movement. (v.7) (Comprehensive study in companion book *Teen Turmoil*, New Leaf Press, Inc. 1988)

--As *evil men and seducers*, they will get worse and worse. (v.13)

Peter writes about the cataclysmic events on earth during the last days:

II Peter 3:10-18

"But the day of the Lord will come as a thief in the night; in the which the heavens shall pass away with a great noise, and the elements shall melt with fervent heat, the earth also and the works that are therein shall be burned up. (v.10)

"Seeing then that all these things shall be dissolved what manner of persons ought ye to be in all holy conversation and godliness, (v.11)

"Looking for and hasting unto the coming of the day of God, wherein the heavens being on fire shall be dissolved and the elements shall melt with fervent heat? (v.12)

"Nevertheless we, according to his promise, look for new heavens and a new earth, wherein dwelleth righteousness. (v.13)

"Wherefore, beloved, seeing that ye look for such things, be diligent that ye may be found of him in peace, without spot, and blameless. (v.14)

"And account that the long-suffering of our Lord is salvation; even as our beloved brother Paul also according to the wisdom given unto him hath written unto you; (v.15)

"As also in all his epistles, speaking in them of these things; in which are some things hard to be understood, which they that are unlearned and unstable wrest, as they do also the other scriptures, unto their own destruction. (v.16)

"Ye therefore, beloved, seeing ye know these things before, beware lest ye also, being led away with the error of the wicked, fall from your own steadfastness. (v.17)

"But grow in grace, and in the knowledge of our Lord and Saviour Jesus Christ. To him be glory both now and forever. Amen." (v.18)

--The *heavens disappear* with a loud *noise*. (v.10)

--The *elements melt* with a fiery heat. (v.10)

--The *earth* will be *destroyed by intense fire*. (v.10)

--Man-made *works* will be *laid bare*. (v.10)

--*Everything* will be utterly dissolved. (Sound like nuclear energy unleashed?) (v.11)

Peter also warns us to be careful about this time:

--The *Lord will come unexpectedly*. (v.12)

--It's time for the believer to get his act cleaned up and get serious about serving God.

--We should *lead holy, devout lives* and *expect* and *help* work for *His imminent return*. (v.14-15)

--We should await His return *blamelessly, growing in grace*. (v.14-18)

A careful reading of all the prophecies of the Bible will not only give the reader an uncanny, complete picture of the "end-times," but it will also accurately describe this period and contemporary society.

Do we know *when* these things will take place?

Although the Rapture, the Second Coming, and the destruction of the earth are predicted by the Bible, the *exact* timetable is not given. The events of Matthew 24, Revelation 18, and Daniel 7 may be geographical, chronological, or overlapping.

The events can begin today, or in 1993, the year 2000, or even later. No one really knows for sure.

The important thing to consider, however, is "How long can we humans keep the planet *safe from annihilation*?" Or "How long will God choose to protect man from himself?" In light of the social, ecological, political, religious, nuclear, and other "corners" we are painting ourselves into, how long do you give mankind?

Will the human race succeed for another thousand years? Or is 500 years a more conservative guess? Perhaps another 100 years?

How about you? Do you think it will last 100 years? Or 50 years? Will we even see the year 2000? It doesn't seem likely.

Only God knows the future, but almost one-third of the content of His Word, the Bible, is prophecy. The Lord intends that His people be clearly informed about the future. He gives all the signs, tells us never to "watch," but to "occupy" (that means to "work"), and to be "ready." That means to be *pure*. He seems to be purging the Church for its last great work; then He will return. "And every man that hath this hope in him purifieth himself, even as he is pure." (I

John 3:3)

The passages that deal with the Second Coming of Jesus Christ make it clear that He will come at a time of unparalleled crisis.

Various passages in the Bible tell us that when we see certain signs or events, this future program is near, "at hand" (Rev. 1:3), "imminent" (Rev. 22:7).

The Second Coming of Christ will be sudden (I Thes. 5:3) and unexpected (Matt. 24:50) and occur at the peak of spiritual wickedness and darkness (I Thes. 5:2-5).

The world will be so caught up in the Humanist-New Age religion/philosophy that they will think that all things are permanently fixed. They will even mock the idea of a Second Coming (II Peter 3:3-4).

Its reality will overtake doubters and atheists with unexpected and destructive results (I Thes. 5:3).

The Second Coming of Christ will be, to the non-believer, a time of eternal catastrophe and condemnation. For the believer it will be a time of joy and celebration for eternity.

We believe that at the end of the Church Age, Satan will produce a great religious and political monolith. The Bible predicts both a *system* and a *person* called the "Antichrist," who will probably be a *political* leader.

The Antichrist will be assisted by a similar personality called the "beast" which is revealed as the "False Prophet," probably a *religious* leader.

Satan, the Antichrist, and the False Prophet will combine in an unholy "trinity" in a final strategy to destroy Israel and God's END-TIME work.

The books of Daniel (Dan. 7-11) and Revelation (Rev. 18) describe the Antichrist as the "man of sin," "man of lawlessness," "son of perdition" (destruction).

The term "man of lawlessness" typifies our age. Disorder, chaos, anarchy, and breakdown characterize every aspect of our modern society.

Jesus told us that the Antichrist would epitomize the character of the world systems of the age and that he would remain a secret until God revealed him.

The "Antichrist's" philosophy is already being disseminated through the HUMANIST REVOLUTION in preparation for his coming. The academic arena could be his world base and source of power and influence. There is a unity of consensus against Bible Faith throughout the Western World in its agencies, unions, programs, and staffs. The "False Prophet" could symbolize a blending of the Apostate Church and the New Age Movement. The high priests could be the rock stars and sensual film idols of the world of entertainment. He will have the attention of the world. How else but through television?

How could a world willingly capitulate to the Antichrist system and leader? The Bible says that initially he will come to solve the crises of the world. The people will willingly give themselves over to the Antichrist and his system.

In fact, secular writers are already clamoring for such a leader. The late Albert Einstein, reflecting on the fact that our world is now small enough for a single nation or terrorist movement to destroy it, said, "The secret of the (nuclear) bomb should be committed to a world government. The world government should have power over all military matters."

Paul M. Mazuer, European economist, wrote:

"The large number of governmental bureaus that will have their orbits in the atmosphere of our planet cannot be allowed to compete and collide with one another. So, in order to control the diverse bureaucracy required, a 'world politiburo' will develop and over this group/organization, there is likely to arise the final and single arbiter - the 'master of the order' - the total dictator."

Harper's magazine carried this quote in an article:

"There will arise 'the man,' strong in character, epigrammatic in manner, personally handsome, continuously victorious; he will sweep aside parliaments, carry civilizations to glory, reconstruct them

171

into an empire and hold (them) together by circulating his profile and organizing further success. He will codify everything, galvanize religion, organize learning into meek academics of little men and women and prescribe a wonderful educational system. And the grateful nations will deify a lucky and aggressive egotism."

A Belgium diplomat who worked with the U.N. said, "We do not want another committee. We have too many already. What we want is a man of sufficient stature to hold the allegiance of all people and to lift us out of the economic morass into which we are sinking. Send us such a man. And be he god or devil, we will receive him."

13

"IN THE LAST DAYS ..."

The condition for the *end* appears to be the proclamation f the Good News of God's Kingdom--that is, the atonement, orgiveness, and redemption of fallen mankind. Matthew 4:14 does not include the word *teach* as part of that condion, only the command to *preach* for a *witness* of the forveness of sin.

Matthew 28:20 says, "Teaching them to observe all ings . . . ." The participle *teaching* means extended, exnded communication as well as learning and growing in blical principles--putting into practice the principles taught "The Great Commandment" (Deuteronomy 6), the Law, d the Prophets, as well as the teachings of the New Testant.

Although this extensive *teaching* is a part of the Great mmission (Matthew 28:20), it (the Great Commission) es not require that every person be taught individually, nor he teaching of every person a condition for the fulfillment the Great Commission. However, the preaching of the spel "in all the world for a witness unto all nations" is necessary for the fulfillment of the Great Commission.

Matthew 24:14 *has* been fulfilled (or will have been by the end of the century), and according to the words of Jesus Christ Himself, *"THEN shall the END come."*

Jesus also encouraged us with the promise, "And, lo, I am with you alway, even *unto the END of the world"* (Matthew 28:20). During the Olivet Discourse the disciples asked Jesus the meaning of *"the END,"* since Jesus used this expression frequently.

Jesus did not mean it would be the *end of everything.* He told the disciples to go out and to *preach* and *teach.* Meanwhile, He would be absent from them. Then, when the time for *"preaching"* and *"teaching"* ends, Jesus will return.

Although Jesus will be absent from the earth during the period of the Church Age, He promised to return at its "end," to be with His followers--"even unto the *end of the world."* The end of the world suggests that this world system, human governments, and man's humanistic influences and activities will end, and God's kingdom will be ushered in upon His return.

His return will mark the end of an age or era--the end of the *"preaching"* and *"teaching"* period, which we call the "Church Age."

When will this happen?

All the *evidence* points convincingly to a time at or around the year 2000. As already pointed out, a host of Christian organizations and leaders have this year as their target. In addition, all the "signs" (fulfilled prophecies) also point to A.D. 2000.

The following is an interesting idea that also seems to fit this chronology. This idea is not a Scriptural nor a theological absolute, but it seems to be appropriate for consideration When we talk about timetables, it is important to know that God has His own agenda. Man marks *time*--a device created in Genesis 1 to allow mankind to keep track of the linear progression of events.

However, "time" does not govern God or His ways. The Apostle Peter wrote, "But, beloved, be not ignorant of this one thing, that one day is with the Lord as a thousand years and a thousand years as one day" (II Peter 3:8). (Incidentally, Peter was also writing about "end-time" events in this chapter.) The Apostle's point was that, to God, *eternity* stands out in stark contrast to time: "*one day* is with the Lord as a *thousand years*."

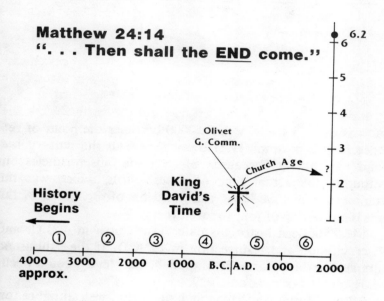

Assuming the time from the Creation to the birth of ~sus Christ to be four "days" of about a thousand years ~ch, and the time *since* Christ two "days" of a thousand ~ars each--the end of this century will symbolically mark ~ix days" of Creation.

The seventh "day" (the day God rested, a "day" of one ~ousand years) will then follow (the "day of the Lord" or ~s millennial reign on earth). After the end of the Church ~e--ending the *"preaching"* and *"teaching"* and the end of ~n's system, as was created in Genesis--the "seven days" ~ be completed.

Creation	Flood	Moses	King David	Christ's Birth	Church Age		Millenium
Day 1	Day 2	Day 3	Day 4	Day 5	Day 6		Day 7
4000	3000	2000	1000	BC/AD	1000	2000	3000

It is easy to see how A.D. 2000 becomes the point of reference in this chronology. However, not all the dates correspond accurately because of various discrepancies in computing the actual time of Jesus' birth, which was the "fulness of *the time*." At this junction of B.C. and A.D., there is an overlap of four to seven years.

Most modern historians date Jesus' birth in 4 B.C. and His crucifixion and resurrection in 29 A.D. If the "thousand years as one day" formula is applied, the "end" could occur as early as 1997 or as late as 2029.

If the Church Age began at Jesus' birth, we can figure two thousand years from Jesus' birth (4 B.C. + 2000 = 1997), less seven years for a premillennial rapture--which puts the date a 1990. However, if the Church Age began at the time of the Great Commission (following Jesus' death and resurrection an before His ascension), the time would be figured from A.D. 2 (29 + 2000 = A.D. 2029), less seven years for premillennia rapture--and the outside date is A.D. 2022.

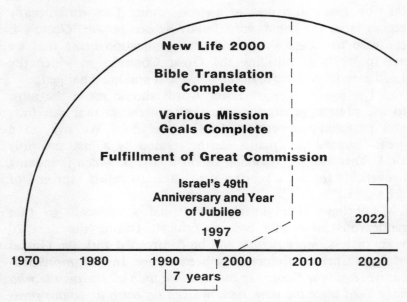

New Life 2000

Bible Translation
Complete

Various Mission
Goals Complete

Fulfillment of Great Commission

Israel's 49th
Anniversary and Year
of Jubilee

1997

2022

1970   1980   1990   2000   2010   2020

7 years

If Rapture here . . . then also Tribulation
. . . then also Armageddon

The final push by Christian agencies to fulfill the Great Commission, and the related signs (in the Mideast) all point to an imminent chronology. When the Jews returned to Palestine in fulfillment of Biblical prophecy, Israel was formed as a nation. As mentioned earlier, this event occurred on May 14, 1948. Israel will celebrate her forty-ninth anniversary on May 14, 1997, which will inaugurate a Jubilee Sabbatical--a full year of celebration and observance that will climax in 1998.

However, to add to what has already been said would be to strain Scriptural credibility. Jesus said, "No man knows the *DAY* nor the *HOUR*." Yet He gave us these many "signs" and then admonished us to watch for them so that when we see "these things coming to pass," we will know He is just offstage ready to enter.

Our responsibility is to "watch" and to "occupy" until He comes. The word *occupy* does not suggest that we are to take up space in a pew or an easy chair. The word *occupy* comes from the same word family as *occupation*. *Occupy* is the verb form for *work*, with the implication being that we are to work at fulfilling the Great Commission which the Lord gave us. We are to *occupy--work* at making it happen.

The significance of Jesus' words should mean the most to the present generation--the first generation that can fully and personally appreciate God's revelation. We live on a great "spaceship," planet Earth, created by a just and holy God. This "craft" is taking us on a voyage which is moving irreversibly toward a rendezvous that Jesus called "the end of the world."

I believe that during the "final approach" to that rendezvous all events become critical. During the next 20 years or less, *more people* will be confronted with the Gospel of Jesus Christ than have ever been before. In fact, *more people will hear the Gospel in our lifetime than all the people who have lived since the time Jesus walked on earth up to our present generation.*

During the brief period ahead, *more children* will receive training from Godly parents and in Christian schools than all the children taught from the creation of the world until 1970, when the Christian school movement began exploding.

This period just before *the end* is also a critical time for believers worldwide to reevaluate their lives. It is a time to reconsider their "occupation," based on the realization of Christ's upcoming return. As with no other previous generation, we need:

> an URGENCY OF COMMITMENT . . .
> an EXPECTATION OF HIS COMING . . .
> and a PURITY OF SERVICE.

A parallel passage records what will take place during this end-time period:

> This know also, that in the last days perilous times shall come.
> II Timothy 3:1

(This passage is treated extensively in the companion volume to this book: TEEN TURMOIL.)

This passage also seems to refer to the 2000-year Church Age period as the "last days." It points out some of the negative and apocalyptic events to come, whereas Peter presents an encouraging picture:

> And it shall come to pass in the last days, saith God, I will pour out of my Spirit upon all flesh: and your sons and your daughters shall prophesy, and your young men shall see visions, and your old men shall dream dreams: and on my servants and on my handmaidens I will pour out in those days of my Spirit; and they shall prophesy; and I will show wonders in heaven above, and signs in the earth beneath; blood, and fire, and vapor of smoke.

Acts 2:17-21

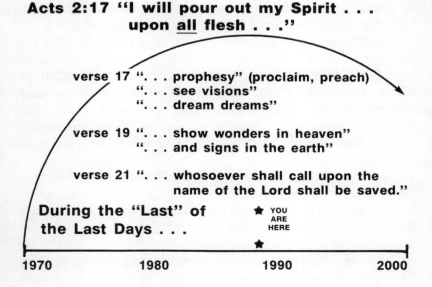

Acts 2:17 "I will pour out my Spirit . . . upon all flesh . . ."

verse 17 ". . . prophesy" (proclaim, preach)
". . . see visions"
". . . dream dreams"

verse 19 ". . . show wonders in heaven"
". . . and signs in the earth"

verse 21 ". . . whosoever shall call upon the name of the Lord shall be saved."

During the "Last" of the Last Days . . .
★ YOU ARE HERE
★

1970   1980   1990   2000

The Apostle Peter preached with great power on the Day of Pentecost, following Jesus' ascension into Heaven. The text which Peter preached from was a prophecy written around 800 B.C. by the Old Testament prophet Joel. Perhaps it was a keynote sermon to usher in a 2000-year Church-Age period. In any event, Peter explained that the people were witnessing a literal fulfillment of Joel's prophecy:

> And it shall come to pass in the *last days*, saith *God, I will pour out* of my Spirit upon all flesh.

Acts 2:17

Then verses 19 through 21 speak of the END-TIME specifically:

> And I will shew wonders in heaven above, and signs in the earth beneath; blood, and fire, and vapour of smoke: The sun shall be turned into darkness, and the moon into blood, before that great and notable day of the Lord come: and it shall come to pass, that whosoever shall call on the name of the Lord shall be saved.

Acts 2:17-21 has a two-fold application. In general, these verses refer to the Church Age. Even more specifically, they refer to the end of the Church Age, or the last of the "last days" (what we describe as from about 1970 to the return of Christ, the rapture of the Church, and subsequent events in or around the year 2000).

Peter says that in the last days, God will pour out His Spirit upon *"all flesh"*--Muslims, Hindus, Buddhists, Catholics, animists, and even Christians. "Your sons and daughters will prophesy," he declares. The word prophesy means to proclaim or preach--*not foretelling* but "forth-telling" the Good News. This passage is a prophetic *revelation* of modern "last days" youth (sons and daughters) caught up in actively fulfilling the Great Commission.

Verse 20 of Chapter Two seems to focus on events which have probably not yet happened, but which are imminent-- with the coming of Jesus Christ at the "time of *the end:*"

> The sun shall be turned into darkness, and the moon into blood, before that great and notable day of the Lord come.

> Acts 2:20

Those who believe in a premillennial, pretribulation rapture of the saints believe this verse describes the awful time to follow, which Jesus also described in Matthew 24 and 25.

Equally significant is the next verse:

> And it shall come to pass, that whosoever shall call on the name of the Lord shall be saved

> Acts 2:21

This is a Church Age principle, and the Apostle Paul expressed it in exactly the same words in Romans 10:13.

Acts 2:17-21 has two meanings and two aspects of fulfillment. One is general and applies to the entire Church Age. The other is uniquely and *significantly* for the generation living in the last of the last days, when young and old alike will be occupied with the primary task of global witnessing. The older men will have the dreams and visions. But it will be the youth, the sons and daughters, who will prophesy and be active in the role given by the Lord Jesus Christ.

This mandate, to me, is crystal clear.

14

GREAT COMMANDMENT/ GREAT COMMISSION

In the spring of 1968, I was driving through the mountains of eastern Kentucky when God gave me a unique vision. As I turned the car to face the horizon where the mountain range was in full view, I saw clearly--as if the words were actually carved in the granite face of the peaks--

"GO START CHRISTIAN SCHOOLS."

These words were not, of course, physically carved in the mountainside--but I was praying, and God put these words indelibly in my mind and heart. I could not lose that vision.

Just as 1968 was a pivotal year for our nation, it was a year of personal struggle for me. At the age of 35, I had already been involved in starting a Christian college--but the call upon my life that I experienced in 1968 was different.

Weeks later, I was in my office with a map of the United States spread before me. As I prayerfully studied the map, I looked down at the state of Texas. Immediately there was a sense of recognition and confirmation:

"GO TO *DALLAS* AND START
CHRISTIAN SCHOOLS."

In the fall of 1968, with the chaos and crumbling of culture all around us, our family settled in Garland, Texas, locating near Dallas Christian Academy where our children could attend school. I served as vice-president of a small university in nearby Plano. During that year I became well acquainted with Dallas Christian Academy and its staff. The following year I was asked to be president of the school.

I spent the 1969-70 school year reacquainting myself with elementary and secondary education. When I went back into the classroom, I found I was working with children who were young scholars as well as those who had learning disabilities. It became clear to me that there was a need for *individualized* education for children. By the end of that year, I found myself preparing a school package and curriculum program that could be implemented in almost every Bible-believing church around the world.

The growing evil influences of the late 60's culture were beginning to have an effect even in Christian homes. More and more parents decided it would be best to separate their children from the world and worldly influences. It was this cultural climate that actually set the stage for an effective Christian school movement.

In September 1970 I rented three rooms in the Miller Road Baptist Church in Garland, Texas, and set up a pilot school for what was to become *Accelerated Christian Education*. From that one local school (where we refined, tested, and developed the system), we began to grow. We created a curriculum, trained others, communicated our concept to the Christian public, and traveled across the nation to promote A.C.E. and to duplicate the system.

In 1971, eight more schools opened. By 1972, there were 87 schools. By 1973, there were 330 A.C.E. schools; in 1974, 550 ; in 1975, 940; in 1976, 1440 ; in 1977, 2000; and in 1978, 2600. Ten years later (in the 1987-88 school year) more than 6000 schools were on the A.C.E. program in 92 countries worldwide.

The impetus of this new school movement and the factors which caused it to grow so dramatically are not mysterious. They are based on Biblical principles, especially those found in the "Great Commandment" (Deuteronomy 6) and in the following Scriptures:

Train up a child in the way he should go.

Proverbs 22:6

Learn not the way of the heathen.

Jeremiah 10:2

Cease, my son, to hear the instruction that causeth to err from the words of knowledge.

Proverbs 19:27

Blessed is the man that walketh not in the counsel of the ungodly, nor standeth in the way of sinners, nor sitteth in the seat of the scornful.

Psalm 1:1

I would have you wise unto that which is good and simple concerning evil.

Romans 16:19

Beware lest any man spoil you through philosophy and vain deceit, after the tradition of men, after the rudiments of the world, and not after Christ.

Colossians 2:8

Finally, brethren, whatsoever things are true . . . honest . . . just . . . pure . . . lovely . . . of good report; if there be any virtue, and if there be any praise, think on these things.

Philippians 4:8

The Christian school movement began to really grow as parents and pastors saw it as a means of providing quality education in an environment that separated youngsters from the world and its influences.

In 1944 Torrey Johnson, Bob Cook, and Billy Graham helped start *Youth For Christ*. This was a para-church effort to reach teenagers for Jesus Christ and disciple them in the faith. YFC created a Saturday night rally to provide alternatives for Christian youth who would otherwise be attracted to worldly events.

In 1951 Bill Bright organized *Campus Crusade for Christ* (another para-church ministry) to provide fellowship for Christians on college and university campuses and to organize and mobilize them to reach other young people. The organization also provided training in discipleship and evangelism.

Both *Youth For Christ* and *Campus Crusade* have been greatly used of God to equip and mobilize youth and young adults. Not only that, hundreds of other great organizations and individual ministries have "spun off" these two significant ministries.

A.C.E. is different. Unlike *YFC* and *Campus Crusade, Accelerated Christian Education* is not a para-church organization. A.C.E. goes directly to churches and gives pastors the tools they need in their *own ministries*, the tools to equip *their own young people* for the future ministries of the local church--"daily in the temple."

During Christmas vacation of 1986, I was studying the Third Great Awakening in the context of the Great Commission and Olivet Discourse. I began to get a fresh appraisal of the whole Christian school movement after 16 years of worldwide development. What I learned troubled me.

Why do we train our youth? We can "train them up in the way they should go," but that still begs an answer to the question *"Why?"*

They can still live and die for self. They can grow up and make a token attempt at some aspect of serving the Church, but for the most part, that is easy. They can still devote much of their time, talents, and wealth to an introverted set of self-sustaining values.

I saw that the Christian school in general was developing an *elitist* mentality and deportment with great athletic aspirations and much orientation concerning jobs and success. The students, to be sure, were being trained. They were getting a good education in sterling academic facilities and environments. They could grow up, go out into the world, make money, and "be successful."

I wondered, "Have we missed the primary function of the Christian school?" My reflections came back time and again to a basic premise--THE GREAT COMMISSION. Several parallel passages explain this important principle and imperative:

> Go ye therefore, and teach all nations, baptizing them in the name of the Father, and of the Son, and of the Holy Ghost: teaching them to observe all things whatsoever I have commanded you: and, lo, I am with you alway, even unto the end of the world.
>
> Matthew 28:19, 20

> . . . Go ye into all the world, and preach the gospel to every creature. He that believeth and is baptized shall be saved; but he that believeth not shall be damned.
>
> Mark 16:15, 16

> And that repentance and remission of sins should be preached in his name among all nations, beginning at Jerusalem. And ye are witnesses of these things. And, behold, I send the promise of my Father upon you: but tarry ye in the city of Jerusalem, until ye be endued with power from on high.
>
> Luke 24:47-49

> But ye shall receive power, after that the Holy Ghost is come upon you: and ye shall be witnesses unto me both in Jerusalem, and in all Judea, and in Samaria, and unto the uttermost part of the earth.
>
> Acts 1:8

Notice this progression of the Great Commission:

> *Believe*
> > *Be baptized*
> > > *Be endued with power*
> > > > *Be witnesses*

Then, for those who *are* witnesses--

> *Go*   *Preach*   *Baptize*   *Teach*

in order that others may

> Believe,
> > Be baptized,
> > > Be endued with power,
> > > > Be witnesses.

There are four verbs in the Great Commission that focus on *repentance* and *remission of sins:*

GOING - PREACHING - BAPTIZING - TEACHING.

These four verbs appear as the key words and get our attention. In the original Greek language of the New Testament, these words are *participles* (progressive forms of the verbs). That is, they tell the action and indicate how it is done, but they *do not focus on the key* to the Great Commission.

There is only *one imperative* in the Great Commission. This imperative, in the various passages of Jesus' words, appears as our "marching order." This one imperative is found in *Matthew 28:19* as a concise directive that condenses all activity into one verb that gives *action, direction, objective, balance,* and *meaning* to the rest.

The key word is *TEACH.* This is not a means of limiting to a style or system of teaching or to "teaching" the Bible. The concept is objective-oriented; *teach* means *disciple*, or *"disciplize,"* or, literally--

Now the heart of the Great Commandment (Deuteronomy 6) was to train up our youth to *love* and *serve* God. This concept was at the heart of the Hebrew worldview and expresses the key difference between the so-called Eastern mentality and our Western mentality.

The Hebrew meaning of Deuteronomy 6 is centered on the responsibility of the parents to develop the *values, lifestyle, character,* and *personality* of their children. Children were taught at an early age that God exists, that He created the universe and everything in it, and that there are absolute standards of behavior based on Biblical laws which God expected them to abide by. Producing children who walked with God was the process that was passed from generation to generation.

Now, for the most part, the Western mentality has been caught up in the world system. Its people have "bought into" the values, lifestyle, character, and personality role models of the *world*.

Westerners expect--even desire--that their children grow up with all the "advantages" of worldliness and the world's system. This is even true of many Christians. They find out, too late, that while they are out *winning the world* through missionary outreach, they are *losing their children* to the world.

The Great *Commandment* is the key to all Old Testament study and understanding. Let me ask you a question. Would God have given the Israelites the Great Commandment--to train up their children "diligently," daily, deliberately, and comprehensively--and then have permitted the Israelites to send their children back down the path into Egypt to attend school?

Would Pharaoh's values, lifestyle, and character have been suitable for the Hebrew children to have as a role model? Would Pharaoh's gods have been all right for the children to follow?

The Great *Commission* is the "great commandment" of the New Testament, the apex of truth and responsibility for the Church Age.

Now, let me ask a second question. Would Jesus have given the Church an all-encompassing responsibility such as the Great Commission--to go and *make disciples* of all the nations and peoples of the earth; to *train people* to *love and serve God* and walk in His ways; to reflect Godly *values, lifestyle, character,* and *personality*--but permit His Church to send their own children *into the world* to be molded by the world, its influences, and its role models?

Of all the people in the world whom followers of the Lord Jesus Christ should be most concerned and dedicated to reaching and discipling, it should be--

THEIR OWN CHILDREN.

How should they do this? Through teaching a life-training system as outlined in Deuteronomy 6:6-25. The Lord God Jehovah *commanded* Jewish families to teach God's ways to their children. This was later endorsed by Jesus in the New Testament (Matthew 22:36-38).

Deuteronomy 6 is a command, not a preference. It is also the key to God's blessing and a means of fulfilling the Great Commission in our own circle.

If we fail to obey the "great commandment" of Deuteronomy 6, *we lose*. We lose our children to the world. Perhaps *forever*.

15

THE CAUSE

A century ago, on August 14, 1885, the fiery preacher and evangelist D. L. Moody presided at a convention in Northfield, Massachusetts. Moody presented a dramatic challenge to the assembled Christian leaders. His remarks were reprinted and widely distributed. Moody's challenge was given to the Church of Jesus Christ:

EVANGELIZE THE WORLD BEFORE 1900.

D. L. Moody observed to his listeners that it was near their meeting place that Jonathan Edwards preached (The Great Awakening), "calling upon disciples everywhere to unite the whole habitable globe."

Moody reminded the people that "mighty revivals of religion followed" and "the spirit of missions was reawakened. . . . In 1792, the first missionary society formed . . . in 1793 William Carey, the pioneer missionary, sailed for India." He reported on the successes of the first "modern" efforts to evangelize the globe.

"And yet the Church of God is slow to move," complained Moody about the response to the Great Commission in his own day. "Millions of the human race are yet without the gospel," he said. He challenged his hearers to help mobilize *ten million* believers (out of 400 "nominal" Christians) to go out and win 100 other souls each, and so forth.

"In the course of the next fifteen years," he encouraged them, "the whole present population of the globe would have heard the good tidings by the year 1900!" (The population at that time was about 1.5 billion.)

Moody referred to the Great Commission (Matthew 24:14) and its fulfillment as a necessary prerequisite for the Lord's Second Coming. He preached, "Peter exhorts us both to *'look for* and *hasten* the coming of the day of God.' " And he wondered, "What if *our inactivity delays His coming?*"

The evangelist appealed to all ministers, missionaries, evangelists, pastors, teachers, and other Christian workers-- as well as "believers of every name" (denominational background). "What a spectacle it would present both to angels and men," he suggested, "could believers of every name, forgetting all things in which they differ, meet . . . sending forth laborers into every part of the world-field!"

Moody concluded his appeal: "It is not by might nor by power, but by the Spirit of the Lord . . . . What we are to do for the salvation of the lost must be done quickly; for the generation is passing away, and we with it."

A year following this convention, Moody held a Bible conference at Mt. Hermon (Northfield, Massachusetts). Two hundred and twenty-one young people attended. Moody challenged them for a 100 percent commitment to the task of reaching the world with the Gospel by 1900. One hundred young people responded, and the famous Student Volunteer Movement began.

Following this conference, the Christian Endeavor movement likewise exploded into churches across America. More than 20,000 young people surrendered their lives to God for missionary service, launching the greatest outreach in response since Jesus gave the Great Commission.

Hundreds of Christian colleges and Bible schools were

founded, along with *tens of thousands of hospitals and clinics* in overseas countries. *Hundreds of thousands* of churches were also planted overseas.

In Moody's time, few medical facilities existed in what are now called "third world" or "developing" countries. *Medical missions* opened up region after region to the Gospel. As the people came to mission clinics and hospitals, they found medical help, but were ministered to spiritually as well. Today, most third world countries have some fairly sophisticated medical services. A number of these countries are experimenting in socialism, therefore, medical assistance from the government is a priority. Even though medical assistance is not available to all, this is not now the greatest perceived need on the mission field.

In addition, since D. L. Moody's time, many of the Catholic and mainline Protestant denominations have become concerned only with the healing of physical ills. Many organizations which were zealous for eternal souls in the past have now lost that vision.

Today, around the world, *people want education*. In the modern world, education equals success. This is a universal maxim that has been promoted since World War II. The popular perception that education opens the door to a better life has been fueled by the "global village" conditions.

Technology has made the world "smaller" and more accessible. English has become the international language of culture and commerce. It is now popularly called the "business language." Eighty percent of all data stored in computers around the world is in the English language. The world is moving into the computer era and a global economy.

For these reasons, people everywhere want an education. Curiously, there is another reason--one which seems too good to be true for Christian missions: people want to *study religion*. There is a growing hunger for truth and for ultimate answers to the growing list of problems of our age. This spiritual hunger is as evident in Iowa as in the Ivory Coast.

A recent publication of the International Institute for Christian Studies, with offices in Salisbury, North Carolina, reports:

Christianity is growing by more than 16,000 persons every day in Africa. The church is exploding with growth in South America and Asia as well.

These facts have been documented in earlier chapters of this book. But what about the *results* of this growth? IICS says this:

> Multiplied thousands of university and college students . . . are waiting to seriously study Christianity
> . . . .

> Many universities find themselves ill-equipped to respond . . . .

> . . . future political, professional and educational leaders . . . do not have the opportunity to seriously investigate Christianity . . . . Many tend to view Christianity as a religion for the poor and uneducated.

These conditions point out the unusual opportunity for Christian missions. *Christian education* is precisely what is called for in the Great Commission. Providing the Gospel to serious inquirers in an educational format, or offering an education in a Christian setting (with a Christian philosophy, based on Biblical principles and values) is a fantastic opportunity. There are a number of ways the Church can do this, and creative people will continue to add to the growing list of possibilities. For years, "tentmakers" have gone overseas as teachers--to Saudi Arabia, China, and other countries closed to missions.

Accelerated Christian Education has already developed educational programs in some 90 different countries around the world. Some of these countries even seek us out to do the job of educating their children because they cannot do it themselves.

This "open door" to missions through education is far superior to that of the medical mission. Missions through education does not require extensive training or expensive equipment, materials, and supplies. Jesus said, "They that are whole have no need of a physician, but they that are sick." Through clinics and hospitals the potential of the harvest was limited to the sick.

But *everyone* needs an education, and that need is not occasional; it is constant for the young and never varies. Not only that, unlike medicine, which creates a door of opportunity for a limited period, education provides an opportunity that is *full time*. Through education, there is access to people for *hours* each day, for at least 12 *years*.

The communists were the first to see this opportunity. The World Awakening is *the* central fact of the second half of the twentieth century. Many of us were alive at the mid-point of this century, and we are aware that the central fact during the middle of the century was *communism*.

We watched as the communist system gobbled up country after country. Those of us who watched entire *continents* fall to communism know the power of education. Their successes may even have given us the false perception that communism is still winning. *It is not!*

Communists are now withdrawing troops from nations they could not subdue; they are backing down to vocal demands in satellite countries, and communist theorists are redefining basic doctrine and methods in China and Russia.

Amazingly, communist countries are even opening doors to Bibles and Christian literature. *Glasnost* and *peristroika* seem like revolutionary ideas to those of us who remember what communism was like under Stalin, Khrushchev, and Mao.

Can it be that, as a result of the World Awakening, Christianity is growing explosively across the world--and communism is dying? *It seems so.*

Communism was thought to be a peril for many countries of the world. South Korea was intimidated by the communist North. Yet, in the 1990's, Korea will be unified, and it is my expectation, based on trends of revival and evangelization thus far, that a sovereign *Christian nation* will eventually emerge.

Likewise, Christianity has a strong base in the Philippines. Central and South America will emerge with strong evangelical churches and equally solid representative governments. In May 1988, Pope John Paul II returned for a second visit through Latin America. His presence bolstered Rome's religious presence there, but also pointed out the influence the evangelical awakening has had on the Catholic Church in Latin America. (Statistics concerning the evangelical influence must have created a lot of anxiety in the Vatican.)

Experts are already predicting that the Soviet "iron curtain" will soon crumble. Gorbachev's policies have awakened in the people a hunger for democratic reforms and values. Russia and her Eastern European satellites will increasingly become trading partners of the West in the European Common Market.

The same is true of Southeast Asia. Western influences have opened these nations so that they can be free countries by the end of the century.

The overall trend in relations between countries is one of growing understanding and self-improvement. (The dark side of this picture is that most of the chaos of *end-time* events will be between Israel and her Muslim or Arab neighbors.)

To many of us, communism has become largely symbolic. Just as Hitler's black swastika had the power to instill fear, so the red flag with hammer and sickle stirs such feelings. However, this is just a symbol of communism--not a definition of it. The same is true of other symbols:

--Russian tanks invading Czechoslovakia.
--Chinese hordes invading Korea.
--May Day parades.
--Viet Cong guerrillas.
--Cuban missiles and Castro.
--Khrushchev and Mao.

These are symbolic of the threat, torture, and cruelty of that power. They are not the power itself--*communism*.

Just what is the mystique of communism? How (and why) could it dominate the lives of so many, command such loyalty to irresolute power, and subdue so much of the world?

When Whittaker Chambers wrote "A Letter To My Children" following World War II, he exposed American communism. "A Letter To My Children" was described as being like shining a light down into a dark well, exposing the awful, slithering creatures as they scurried for cover.

Chambers, himself, had turned from darkness to light. He broke with communism and became a Christian. He explained his actions in testimony before the House Committee on Un-American Activities:

> I repudiated Marx's doctrines and Lenin's tactics. . . . . Experience and the record had convinced me that communism is a form of totalitarianism and that its triumph means slavery to men whenever they fall under its sway . . . .

Whittaker Chambers became a witness against communism while Christianity was still on the decline and Western civilization was crumbling. He wrote this statement:

> A man is not primarily a witness *against* something. That is only incidental to the fact that he is a witness *for* something. A witness . . . is a man whose *life* and *faith* are *so completely one* that when he is challenged to step out and testify for his faith, he does so, disregarding all risks, accepting all consequences.

(This statement is one of the best definitions describing the demands of the Great Commission for believers.)

Before a grand jury in New York, Chambers was asked, "What does it mean to be a communist?" His answer was simple, yet obvious. Yet it has eluded the Christian and Western world for years.

We are intrigued by the nature of communism and the source of its power. Why? Perhaps it is because *communism is the antithesis of the Great Commission.*

Every Christian should read Chambers' 1952 book *Witness*, especially the introductory section entitled "A Letter To My Children," wherein he sets forth this antithesis.

What *was* the power behind that "great force," as he describes communism?

Did people become communists because they were morally depraved? No. In fact, many become communists for moral reasons.

Because they were duped or ignorant? No. Many communists are well-educated and are intellectuals.

Then how is it that this idea, espoused mostly by political outcasts, has become the immense force that has mastered much of mankind?

To really understand communism, it is important to understand what it is *not*. Communism has been caricatured by the West and its threat reduced to simplistic slogans.

Communism is *not* "a vicious plot hatched by evil men." It is *not* "the pernicious writings of Marx and Lenin." It is *not* "the labor theory of value, or the strike."

Neither is communism the Red Army, secret police, labor camps, conspiracies, or brainwashing. As Whittaker Chambers explains, "These are expressions of communism, but they are *not* what communism is about."

Then, what *is* communism? What is a communist? What is the *power* behind what we perceive as a satanic system that is the political antithesis of the Great Commission?

Chambers says it is simple to understand. He quotes Karl Marx: "Philosophers have *explained* the world; it is necessary for *you to change the world*."

Whittaker Chambers states:

Communists are bound together by no secret oath. The tie that binds them across the barriers of language and differences of class and education, in defiance of religion, morality, truth, law, honor, the weakness of the body and irresolutions of the mind, even unto death, is a simple conviction: it is necessary to **change the world**.

The power behind communism is the *"power* to hold *convictions* and to *act* upon them."

Communism is the greatest counterfeit religion of all time. As an antithesis of the Great Commission, it can only be the work of Satan to keep men from learning the truth about God, Jesus Christ, redemption, the optimism of the Atonement, and eternal life. But in the last days God is pouring out His spirit upon "all flesh"--even communist nations.

Communists succeeded because they gave people a *cause.* But the cause was empty, self-serving, and a counterfeit of God's best.

Communists have already proven that it is possible to change the world. They did it through EDUCATION--with a counterfeit to the Great Commission. Now, we must have the same dedication to *our cause*--to *change the world* and to do it *in this generation*, while there is still time. We must give our Christian youth the power to hold *convictions* and to *act* upon them.

The great *curse* of the contemporary Christian School movement is that an entire generation of Christian young people (and their parents) have carried their Rational Humanism into their schools. They have been captured by the affluence of this age, by an elitist mentality, and by the desire for education as a *means to the wrong end*--a good job, money, and "success."

Curiously, communists bemoan that their youth are quite similar.

No one is left committed to the cause. Communism is dying; and in the Laodicean Church today *The Cause* seems to elude us.

What is needed is for local churches and Godly parents to instill in our youth a *cause*: the power to hold *convictions* and to *act* upon them--

TO WIN OUR WORLD FOR JESUS CHRIST
IN THIS GENERATION.

This *cause* must be so all-encompassing that a person's life and faith are one, and when the challenge comes to testify for his faith, he does so without question.

Christian youth, who are committed to the Lord Jesus Christ, who believe in Biblical convictions and values, and who are willing to "disregard any risks and accept all consequences" for their faith--Christian youth who are motivated by a Higher Cause and a Greater Power.

CAN AND *WILL* CHANGE THE WORLD!

A massive educational thrust to fill the vacuum of educational needs in the third world can give their contemporary church youth a major *cause* which is the very substance of the GREAT COMMISSION.

On a recent trip to Guatemala, where 33 percent of the people now profess Christ as Savior, I preached in a church for the main Sunday morning service (9 a.m.). The auditorium was packed to capacity, with people standing from wall to wall and down the aisle, as well as in the foyer. There were only a half-dozen cars parked outside; people walked to the 7 a.m., 9 a.m., 11 a.m., 2 p.m., and 5 p.m. services. The 4000-member church also has a Christian school, and the people are becoming inspired to send out missionaries from their own congregation.

As my host and intrepreter George Serrano Elias (who is likely to be the next president of Guatemala) and I rode down the street, he pointed out new churches. He showed me an old skating arena where a Bible-believing church now meets. He also pointed out a disco that had gone bankrupt that is now the building of a great church.

We drove to a new church for the 11:00 service and were greeted in a packed facility by over 1000 worshipers. This church has a newly established Christian school. The Great Commission and Christian education are indivisible during a revival or awakening.

The CONGRESO INTERNATIONAL Para La EVANGELIZACION DEL MUNDO LATINO conducted in July of 1988 at the Anaheim Convention Center attracted over 5000 pastors of all evangelical labels. Many of those attending were from Spain and Central and South America. At the opening rally 2500 laymen and spectators were turned away because of lack of space. Leading pastors and evangelists conducted many general sessions and workshops. The Accelerated Christian Education School of Tomorrow booth was full whenever the people were moving into or out of the sessions. Key pastors from many Latin countries explained that they had come looking for Christian school material and curriculum which they could take back to their countries. Most were not aware that a school program like A.C.E. is being translated and can provide bilingual Christian education with computer-enhanced learning.

These pastors are perceptive and have a *cause*. They know that the awakening will run its course within a decade or so in the Church. They also know that if they can bring educational reform, it could last well into the next century and generation.

Christians in awakening countries want Christian education. They want English education. They want computerized education. To provide this, Western Christianity simply needs the tools and *A CAUSE*--the same cause which D. L. Moody stressed in the Church in the late 1800's: "The Spirit of missions has reawakened. . . . Could believers of every name, forgetting all things in which they differ, meet sending forth laborers into every part of the world-field."

People want education. They want to study Christianity. They want to learn English. They want to be computer literate. Ironically, today even Communist countries who once exported their communism through education are wanting these same cultural assets. This can all be provided by the Church through the power of EDUCATION-- "CHRISTIAN" EDUCATION. Now the CAUSE--to change the world through education--is in the hands of the Church.

16

MOBILIZATION

Evangelist D. L. Moody was able to evoke a sense of commitment to the Great Commission at the apex of industrial progress in the late nineteenth century. Commitment began with a small cadre of young people attending Moody's Mt. Hermon Bible Conference in 1886 and grew to a worldwide force of 20,000 missionaries who spearheaded the greatest evangelistic outreach for the Gospel since the time of the apostles.

On the heels of the current Third Great Awakening, *what* will be the by-product for continued evangelism and missions outreach?

Contemporary Church leaders look at the Christian school movement and rejoice at what God has done. But a follow-up question pleads answer: what is the most significant factor which the current Christian school movement provides for the Church community? It is not its sports program, quality academics, superior discipline, nor even its separation from worldly influences.

The most *significant* contribution of the Christian school

movement to the Church community is its youth. Only Christian schools can provide the leadership to train and disciple youth to love and serve God. Plus, they have the youth itself to become the mission force of the immediate future.

Christian school children currently make up at least five percent of the nation's youth. Today's young people are available, accessible, and capable of being trained and mobilized on a day-to-day basis even more than they were in Moody's era.

Conservatively, at least 20,000 Christian schools are already in place around the world. Over *200,000 teenagers* in these Christian schools will graduate within the next three years.

These young people could be the "strike force" to spearhead an outreach into underdeveloped nations of the world. Their weapon? It is something that can *touch* every life in the world by the year 2000: *education* geared to the principles of the Great Commission--to *"MAKE DISCIPLES."* Just as Moody's "Christian Endeavor" force of 20,000 young people made an impact on the world, so the children of the World Awakening can change nations on this planet forever.

During the decade from January 1, 1989, to January 1, 1999, Christian schools will graduate at least a *half-million young people*. For what purpose? What will be their cause--their goal? More education? A job? Marriage and materialism? How will they spend their lives until Christ returns?

There are presently 40,000 teenagers in *Accelerated Christian Education* schools. Over 100,000 will graduate by the year 2000. They will grow up imbued with a Biblical philosophy of life, a sense of responsibility for their own learning, a high level of Christian character, and an outstanding academic education (usually three years ahead of their peers in public schools).

Even these benefits are not enough. Young people need a *Cause* in which they can invest their lives.

The goal for the Church of the 1990's is the *mobilization* of a potential force of 100,000 young people. To that objective the responsibility of every evangelical and fundamentalist Church school leader is clear. That responsibility is to give our young people the *highest purpose* for living--to *love God* and to serve Him on a practical day-to-day basis.

Together, we must (as Moody said) abandon those things that divide us and concentrate on those which unite us. Here is a suggested agenda:

1. Prepare your young people to be involved in the *end-time harvest*.
2. Help them adopt and act on *a world vision*. (They could begin by reading this book.)
3. Encourage them to make a *personal commitment* to *involvement in the Great Commission*.
4. Involve them in a *Cause*--to *change the world* for the Lord Jesus Christ.
5. Provide them with the *tools to do the job*.

What are the tools to be used in reaching this last generation of Planet Earth? There is an obvious answer. Simply look at several *trends*:

--Every month the world grows by "two Chicagos" (16 million).

--Every month India grows by 1.3 million (more than the population of Nebraska).

--During the next decade the world will grow by *one billion* (the population of China).

--We live in a *younger* world (40 percent of the world today is under the age of 15).

--By the year 2000, school-aged children will make up almost half the world's population.

If we superimpose these trends on the three basic human ants being expressed worldwide (especially in third world ations), the method of reaching the world for Christ comes self-evident:

1. People want education.
2. People want to learn English.
3. People want to learn about Christianity.

Because the Chinese people want to learn English, the door to the largest nation in the world has opened to the Gospel. Christian teachers can help fulfill the desire of the Chinese to learn English.

India, the world's second largest nation, believes that education is the most important thing a person can acquire. Moreover, India wants its youth educated in English. They do not even object if it is in a Christian context.

There are 370,000 villages in India without schools. That door is wide open. Dr. Rochunga Pudaite of India reports that in nearly every village where a school has been started, a Christian Church opens soon after.

The continent of Africa has as many people as India and as many villages without schools. A.C.E.'s mail requesting help in starting schools is heaviest from Africa.

By the year 2000, sixty percent of the world's Christians and many missionaries will be from third world countries where Christian mission programs will not provide enough Christian schools, Bible colleges, seminaries, and Christian training centers to train their youth. As the third world looks for assistance, Christian schools can give them all they need. A.C.E. has a package, an educational system, that will *"make disciples"* of future leaders for "all nations, tribes and peoples."

A.C.E. youth know how to do it. They have been in A.C.E. Learning Centers. With a little additional training, they can reproduce A.C.E. "training centers" in nations around the world. They can help fulfill the Great Commission and change the WORLD by helping untrained national pastors in foreign countries to set up schools and provide

1. Education.
2. English.
3. Information about Christianity.
4. Upper-level Bible college programs.

The general solution, then, is to mobilize youth of existing Christian schools to become the final effective missionary force through Christian education for the end-time harvest of the Great Commission.

But a practical question remains. How can that be accomplished?

The following is by no means an exhaustive plan, but it can serve as an outline for an immediate mobilization strategy to "Make Disciples" of *your* young people so they will want to "Make Disciples" of others:

1. Turn Off the Television.

"Making Disciples" is a *separation* movement. Television, worldly magazines and music, and other secular influences dilute Biblical influence and prevent *loving* and *serving* God. They are also major contributors to "Laodiceanism" within the Church. Many Christian families have gotten rid of their televisions because of the negative influence on family life.

2. Study the Bible.

The passages that need a great deal of consideration include the "Great Commandment" (Deuteronomy 6), the "Great Commission" (Matthew 28:19, 20; Mark 16:15, 16; Luke 24:46-49; and Acts 1:8), the Gospels, and the book of Acts. Specific "how-to" information can be found in the Gospels and the book of Acts. A Bible study for young people may be led on "How to Change the World."

3. Pray--and Teach Students to Pray.

A leader or parent must lead by example. Make prayer an important part of daily life. Spend time every day on your face before God in prayer for your children and students, for their preparation and future, and for your students' families. Regular prayers and personal devotions by the students are significant times of spiritual growth. Special "Day of Prayer" emphasis or regular prayer exercises are also important. "Pray ye therefore the Lord of the harvest, that he will send forth labourers into his harvest" (Matthew 9:38).

4. Teach Students to Love God.

Teach the Great Commandment as the first duty of man: " . . . love the Lord with *all thine heart . . . .*" Memorize key Old and New Testament passages that show what it means to give God first place and to have an obsession with God and His will (use Biblical examples of loving and walking with God). Use these Biblical examples in sermons. Teach the young people to have a quiet place where they can be alone with God. Teach them to walk with Him. Commit to "Make Disciples" who will first and foremost love God.

5. Study Other Revivals and Awakenings.

Increase awareness and consciousness of the Great Awakening, Second Great Awakening, famous Welsh Revival, and Indonesian Revival. Read books such as *Like a Mighty Wind, On the Crest of the Wave, "Intercessor," Peace Child,* and *Eternity In Their Hearts.* Read biographies of Moody, Finney, and Whitefield. (Devotions and chapel readings from these books will inform, challenge, and inspire.)

6. Train Students to Witness.

Teach them a simple plan like the "Four Spiritual Laws," or have them take the A.C.E. Soul Winning PACE. Take them to witness in shopping malls and on door-to-door visitation, to visit the sick in nursing homes and hospitals, and so on. A *disciple* is a *witness*.

7. Teach Students to Serve God.

To "Make Disciples" is the ultimate objective. From preschool, through ABC's, through elementary and secondary schools, a disciple must *choose* to serve God. The philosophy of "full-time *Christian work*," as opposed to *secular* work, is humanistic. A child should be taught from his earliest years to be a disciple; he should be taught that he is not his own and that he must "live for God." Commitment should be sought from the earliest years.

A child should be challenged to give his life to serve God with the understanding that some day God will direct his steps into the specific work He wants him to do. He should be taught to serve God and use every opportunity to witness regardless of the vocation to which God calls him. Even as a child, he should be encouraged to make it his life objective to become a disciple and to change the world for God. Whether he does this in a Church-related position or in another vocational field is up to God--one is no more spiritual than the other if he is where God wants him. What makes his work "Christian" is his lifestyle and commitment.

One of the largest evangelical denominations sends one out of every 2025 of its members into missions; the Mormons send one out of every 96 members. Of those Mormons who go overseas to serve, 99 percent become leaders in the movement. The Church of Jesus Christ of Latter Day Saints is considered to be the fastest growing religion in the world. Their lowest church growth rate for a decade was 28 percent. During the 1970's they grew by 58 percent, and during 1986 their total membership passed six million, with 42,000 on the mission field.

The following insights were shared by Mr. Archie Perez, a former Mormon:

--The Mormon Church encourages and fosters in children an anticipation for the day they become missionaries.

--Training is not for scholarly pursuits but for the practical aspects of enlisting, converting, and training nations in Mormonism.

--Each missionary raises his own support; he is responsible from start to finish. Success enhances his self-image and his confidence in the Church as his reference point for his future self-esteem.

--The time for a Mormon's two years of service is during the transition between high school and college or vocational commitment.

--The two years of service leave them well-grounded in their faith and commit them indefinitely to missions, either to continue as a missionary or to support missions as a church leader at home.

8. Take Students to Conferences and Conventions.

Expose young people and their leaders to Christian school conventions, Bible conferences, and other events where they can learn and interact. Both will catch the vision for service and want to share it.

9. Let Youth Meet Real Missionaries.

When they hear missionary speakers (or better yet, talk personally with missionaries), young people relate much better to experiences of missionaries and learn how God calls people into particular service opportunities.

10. Teach the Subject of Missions.

Where are the fields opening? What "harvest

areas" are already ripe? What are the various mission agencies and their needs? How does one prepare for cross-cultural missions service? (It is not overreaching for the students to be exposed to this for one hour daily--maybe in devotions or Bible class.)

11. Plan Projects for Missions.

Students can plan the projects themselves and become involved with actual missionaries from various fields. Maps and globes can be used in teaching the geographical locations of missionaries.

Students should use pencils for writing in PACE's; the PACE's can then be sent (duty-free) to schools overseas where they can be erased and reused on the mission field.

Students can display photos, drawings, and maps in their offices regarding missions and missionaries. (Do not forget *home* missions as well as foreign missions.)

12. Periodically Present a Challenge.

--Challenge them to serve God in a ministry capacity at home or abroad.
--Challenge them to spend one or two years as short-term missionaries at home or abroad (preferably to build Christian schools for other children).
--Challenge them to attend Christian colleges or Bible schools.

Stress the importance of these challenges and encourage *their* input and ideas.

13. Help Them Catch a Personal Vision.

It is not enough that they simply "play back"

your dreams of service. They must *personalize* the dreams and *identify* with the needs. In so doing, they will *catch their own vision* for service.

14. Teach Them How to Listen for God's Voice.

God leads through His Word, through Godly preaching, and through wise counsel of parents, pastors, teachers, and others. Encourage personal "quiet times" and daily journal entries where they record what they believe God is leading them to do with their lives.

15. Teach Their Parents.

It is important that these same principles of discipleship be taught and explained to the parents of your students. Parents who know your aims can reinforce them. These same principles should likewise be included in sermons and presented at youth and parent-teacher fellowships.

16. Organize a "His Servants' Club."

For students committed to serve God, a "His Servants' Club" can be the most significant method of involvement and planning. The club should be open to those who take the initiative to commit their lives to God. The club should meet at least once a week, or when there is a need (such as a project that needs to be done).

A concerned and committed staff member should serve as director or counselor. Developing a Godly character and serving God should be held in highest esteem instead of sports or academics.

17. Plan and Carry Out "His Servants' Club" Activities.

a. Work on projects for missionaries.

b. Participate in a fall or spring school revival.

c. Promote Christian schools in other churches (with the pastor or principal).

d. Work with younger students (a practical Paul-Timothy approach).

e. Start an exchange program with other "His Servants' Clubs" for chapel or assembly.

f. Encourage a breakfast, lunch, or dinner meeting with each guest missionary or chapel speaker.

18. **Plan Other Possibilities for "His Servants' Club" Participation.**

a. Students could take an annual trip to a mission field. The group could come to A.C.E. for orientation and then drive into Mexico for a week of service in a local school or church.

b. The school could set up special awards for students who demonstrate commitment to serve God. (Suggestions: award pins, membership card, logo, distinctive blazer, special activities and social events, etc.)

c. **International Training Program (Internship)**
Upon graduation from high school, students could participate in overseas missionary service:
--They would spend a summer at A.C.E. headquarters in Texas for orientation, training, and planning. They would be teamed with a partner.

--They would spend the fall in their home school as a monitor, working under the supervision of the pastor or principal and getting "hands-on" experience as educators.

--They would then get commitment from home, friends, and relatives for financial and prayer support.

--At the appropriate time, they would go to the field (two by two), accompanied by a pastor who has A.C.E. experience and training.

--The "A.C.E." pastor (staying two or three weeks) would then train the local national pastor and staff and help them begin a school there on the field.

--The students would stay for the remainder of the school year, or as long as visas permit.

In 1988 I received a letter from I. T. Taguchi, principal of Yokoham Christian Academy in Japan. It was in response to my scheduled workshop on the fall convention tour addressing the subject of "Mobilizing Our Youth." In agreement with our concept, Mr. Taguchi wrote:

The Lord has directed us not to use the school as an ivory tower, but to train our students to go out to assault the powers of darkness. With the help of God we have done this. . . . God has opened many doors in many areas such as a Catholic orphanage, a Buddhist kindergarten, English classes, military bases, and parks. . . . The children themselves have developed some creative ways to evangelize. . . . God has given us over 100 salvations through these outreaches."

Again, we do *not* build Christian schools primarily to give a child the best education *nor teach him how to make a good living*. Teaching him *how to live* and *to love and serve God* are our primary tasks.

Christian schools should not attach the same significance to expensive athletic programs as public schools. *Spiritual* training is of primary significance. In fact, it would be better *not to have* a sports program if you have to choose between it and mobilizing your youth to live for God. Building Godly character and Biblical values is of much greater importance!

Likewise, the *primary* function of the Christian school is not to prepare students to go on to secular state universities or colleges. There are many Christian colleges and universities where students can prepare for a career while learning in a Godly environment.

The Apostle Paul wrote, "Beware lest any man spoil you through philosophy and vain deceit, after the tradition of men, after the rudiments of the world, and not after Christ" (Colossians 2:8). This admonition is not only applicable to elementary schools; it is even more critical for higher education.

Christian education is not simply a good alternative. It is the *only Biblical way* for Christians to prepare their children for life. It has always been "the only way."

However, the current generation of adults has been "trained up in Egypt" and spent years struggling in the wilderness finally to see how critical Bible training really is. Sometimes we are too late to save our own children. Laodiceanism grips the Church in the last of the last days. This affects our attitude of responsibility toward our children.

Christian education is the only way to pass along to our children Godly faith, Biblical values and principles, character, and the desire to love and serve God. Have you ever heard of a public school accomplishing this?

Christian education is also the only way to quickly and efficiently *mobilize a generation* around a supreme Cause. Christian schools make possible and reasonable our goal to complete the fulfillment of the Great Commission in *this generation*, perhaps even before the year 2000. Starting a Christian school brings the children into the church--"daily in the temple"--for full-time Christian training for preparation and mobilization.

The worldwide Great Awakening is the *positive* motivation for this important and critical task.

The Bible also gives a *negative* motivation, and perhaps its focus is even more critical:

> "This know also, that in the last days perilous times shall come."
>
> II Timothy 3:1

For facts about Western culture and its decadent influence on our children, and for information on what we can do about it--read the companion book to this volume (also published by New Leaf Press):

TEEN TURMOIL.

APPENDIX

TOOLS FOR CHRISTIAN SCHOOLS:

Chapel Activities,

HIS SERVANTS' CLUBS,

Church Youth Retreats,

Etc.

Compiled by Larry Sauvageot

MEETING OUTLINE

A general outline for a monthly chapel service, a meeting of "His Servants' Club," a youth retreat, a special Saturday night meeting, and so forth, for the mobilization of youth for full-time Christian service.

THEME: (A list of possible themes follows outline.)

MEMORY VERSE: Mark 16:15

SONGS: Choose two or three good missions songs. (A list of sources is included in this Appendix.)

OFFERING: Use little school houses and put in a container with a picture of a big schoolhouse.

If individual record of giving is used, little school houses can be placed in container and offering counted later.

INCENTIVES: Boys against girls contest
Level against level

REWARDS: Ten-minute break for winners
Ribbons for top boy and girl
Recognize top givers at Awards night

STORY: Choose one from list included in this Appendix or use one of your own choice. A continued story like *Hudson Taylor* by Child Evangelism Fellowship (five parts) works very well.

THEMES

The following are suggested themes to be used in the meeting; the themes have a missions emphasis. The suggested gifts can be distributed to each student or just to the top givers. Build curiosity and interest by just emphasizing the theme and letting the students guess what the gifts will be. There is a Resource List included in this Appendix which gives a list of the companies from which you may order the gifts.

"SHARPEN UP FOR MISSIONS"
(gift: pencil sharpeners)

"MISSIONS IS MUSIC TO THE EARS"
(gift: kazoos)

"DISCOVER THE WORLD THROUGH MISSIONS"
(gift: globe key chains)

"TAKE NOTE FOR MISSIONS"
(gift: little note pads)

"GIVING TO MISSIONS IS FANTASTIC"
(gift: paper fans)

"PUT YOUR HEART IN MISSIONS"
(gift: heart-shaped balloons)

"GIVING TO MISSIONS IS THE RULE"
(gift: rulers)

"SPRING INTO MISSIONS"
(gift: kites or slinkies)

"UP, UP, AND AWAY FOR MISSIONS"
(gift: Bible story balloons or Frisbees)

"LET THE SON SHINE IN"
(gift: sun visors or sunglasses)

"GIVING IS NO PUZZLE THROUGH MISSIONS"
(gift: small puzzles of any type)

SUGGESTED STORIES

"Bold Bearers of His Name" by William N. McElrat, Broadman Press (40 world missions stories)

"I Dare," Child Evangelism Press (Five-part story of Amy Carmichael)

"Hudson Taylor," Child Evangelism Press (Five-part biography)

"Madugu," Child Evangelism Press (The true story of a Nigerian boy)

"Run, Ma, Run," Child Evangelism Press (Biography of Mary Slessor, a great missionary leader in Africa)

"A Miracle for Samuelito," Bible Visuals Inc. (A visualized story of Mexico)

(Check your Bible bookstore for more.)

RESOURCE LIST

Inexpensive Gifts and Promotions

Oriental Merchandise
2636 Eden Born Avenue
Metairie, Louisiana 70002

Palmer Sales
P. O. Box 247
Mesquite, Texas 75149

U.S. Toys Company, Inc.
1927 East Beltline Road
Carrollton, Texas 75006

Stories

International Associated Missionaries Inc.
4305 S.W. 60th Street
Fort Lauderdale, Florida 33314

Child Evangelism Fellowship
P.O. Box 348
Warrenton, Missouri

Broadman Press

Bible Visuals, Inc.
Box 2
Akron, Pennsylvania 17501-0153

SIM USA
P.O. Box 7900
Charlotte, North Carolina 28217

BCM International, Inc.
237 Fairfield Avenue
Upper Darby, Pennsylvania 19082

Songs

Child Evangelism Fellowship
P.O. Box 348
Warrenton, Missouri

Sacred Literatures Ministries
Box 777
Taylors, South Carolina 29687-0777

Non-Denominational Mission Society Magazines

ACMC Newsletter
Association of Church Missions Committees
1021 East Walnut, Suite 202
Pasadena, CA 91106

Action Report
Language Institute for Evangelism
P.O. Box 200
Alhambra, CA 91802

The Andean Outlook
Andes Evangelical Mission
508 Central Avenue
Plainfield, NJ 07060

Asian Report
Asian Outreach
G.P.O. Box 13448
HONG KONG

Bread for the World Newsletter
207 East 16th Street
New York, NY 10003

Broadcaster
Far East Broadcasting Company
P.O. Box 1
Whittier, CA 90608

Brown Gold
New Tribes Mission
Woodworth, WI 53194

China and the Church Today
Chinese Church Research Center
1564 Edge Hill Road
Abington, PA 19001

Church Growth Bulletin
Overseas Crusades, Inc.
P.O. Box 66
Santa Clara, CA 95050

CMF Record
Carver Foreign Missions, Inc.
Morris Brown Sta., Box 92091
Atlanta, GA 30314

Communique and Ambassadors
Ambassadors for Christ, Inc.
P.O. Box AFC
Paradise, PA 17562

Compassion Magazine
Compassion, Inc.
7774 W. Irving Park Road
Chicago, IL 60634

The Cross and the Crescent
North Africa Mission
239 Fairfield Avenue
Upper Darby, PA 19082

Deaf Witness
Christian Mission for Deaf Africans
P.O. Box 1452
Detroit, MI 48231

Doorways (quarterly)
International Students
P.O. Box C
Colorado Springs, CO 80906

East Asia Millions
Overseas Missionary Fellowship
404 South Church Street
Robesonia, PA 19551

Evangelizing Today's Child
Child Evangelism Fellowship, Inc.
P.O. Box 348
Warrenton, MO 63383

Everybody
World Literature Crusade
20232 Sunburst Street
Chatsworth, CA 91311

FAX
Food for the Hungry, Inc.
P.O. Box 200
Los Angeles, CA 90041

Floodtide (quarterly)
Christian Literature Crusade, Inc.
P.O. Box C
Fort Washington, PA 19034

Focus
Missionary Internship, Inc.
P.O. Box 457
Farmington, MI 48024

Focus News
International Students, Inc.
P.O. Box C
Colorado Springs, CO 80906

Global Church Growth Bulletin
Overseas Crusades
3033 Scott Boulevard
Santa Clara, CA 95050

Global Report
World Evangelical Fellowship
P.O. Box 670
Colorado Springs, CO 80401

GO and *LINK*
Bible and Medical Missionary Fellowship
P.O. Box 418
Upper Darby, PA 19082

Gospel in Context: A Focus on the Contextualization of the
Gospel in the Six Continents
1564 Edge Hill Road
Abington, PA 19001

Greater Europe Report
Greater Europe Mission
P.O. Box 668
Wheaton, IL 60187

Harvest Today
World Team
Box 343038
Coral Gables, FL 33134

Harvest
Baptist Mid-Missions
4205 Chester Avenue
Cleveland, OH 44103

In Other Words
Wycliffe Bible Translators
19891 Beach Boulevard
Huntington Beach, CA 92648

In Touch
IFES
10 College Rd., Harrow
Middlesex HA1 1BE
ENGLAND

Inland Africa
Africa Inland Mission
P.O. Box 178
Pearl River, NY 10965

Intercessor (monthly prayer bulletin)
Mission Aviation Fellowship
P.O. Box 2828
Fullerton, CA 92633

International Viewpoint (monthly)
Christian Literature Crusade, Inc.
P.O. Box C
Fort Washington, PA 19034

Inter-Seminary Student Missions Newsletter
P.O. Box 13053
Portland, OR 97213

JEMS
Japan Evangelical Mission
P.O. Box 640, Three Hills
Alberta, Canada

Latin America Evangelist
Latin America Mission
285 Orchard Terrace
Bogota, NJ 07603

Lifeline
Unevangelized Fields Mission
P.O. Box 306
Bala-Cynwyd, PA 19004

Link
Interlink
Box 832
Wheaton, IL 60187

Map Miniature Magazine (quarterly)
Map Progress (quarterly)
Map International
P.O. Box 50
Wheaton, Il 60187

Message of the Cross
Bethany Fellowship Missions
6820 Auto Club Road
Minneapolis, MN 55438

Missiology: An International Review
American Society of Missiologists
1605 E. Elizabeth
Pasadena, CA 91104

Mission Aviation (quarterly)
Mission Aviation Fellowship
P.O. Box 2828
Fullerton, Ca 92633

Mission Frontiers
U.S.Center for World Mission
1605 E. Elizabeth Street
Pasadena, CA 91106

Missions Advance Research and Communication Newsletter
World Vision/MARC
919 W. Huntington Drive
Monrovia, CA 91109

Newsletter
Daystar Communications, Inc.
P.O. Box 10123
Eugene, OR 97401

Newsletter
TransWorld Radio
560 Main Street
Chatham, NJ 07928

Occasional Bulletin
Overseas Ministries Study Center
P.O. Box 443
Fort Lee, NJ 07024

O.M. News (quarterly)
Operation Mobilization
P.O. Box 148
Midland Park, NJ 07432

OMS Outreach
O.M.S. International, Inc.
P.O. Box A
Greenwood, IN 46142

The Other Side: A Magazine of Christian Discipleship
(Not actually a mission society, but good perspectives on
world trends and needs.)
Box 12236
Philadelphia, PA 19144

Outlook
African Enterprise, Inc.
P.O. Box 988
Pasadena, CA 91102

Pray for China Prayer Bulletin
Pray for China Fellowship
1423 Grant Street
Berkeley, CA 94703

Prayer Fellowship Bulletin (monthly)
Regions Beyond Missionary Union
8102 Elberon Avenue
Philadelphia, PA 19111

Prayer Letters (weekly)
Operation Mobilization
P.O. Box 148
Midland Park, NJ 07432

Prayer News Bulletin
Fellowship of Faith for the Muslims
205 Yonge St., Rm. 25
Toronto, Ontario
CANADA M5B 1N2

Regions Beyond (quarterly)
Regions Beyond Missionary Union
8102 Elberon Avenue
Philadelphia, PA 19111

Reporter
World Relief Commission, Inc.
P.O. Box 44
Valley Forge, PA 19481

SCAN: A Six Continent Reading Service for the Renewal of
Church and Mission
1564 Edge Hill Road
Abington, PA 19001

Slavic Gospel News
Slavic Gospel Association, Inc.
P.O. Box 1122
Wheaton, IL 60187

Student World Report
IFES
233 Langdon Street
Madison, WI 53703

Student and World Connection
Inter-Varsity Missions
233 Langdon Street
Madison, WI 53703

Themelios
Theological Students Fellowship
233 Langdon Street
Madison, WI 53703

Today's Christian
Fuller Evangelistic Assoc.
Box 989
Pasadena, CA 91102

20th Century Disciple
Youth With A Mission, Inc.
P.O. Box 1099
Sunland, CA 91040

Update
Presbyterian Center for Missions Studies
1605 E. Elizabeth
Pasadena, CA 91104

Update (World Concern)
Box 33000
Seattle, WA 98133

Wherever
The Evangelical Alliance Mission
P.O. Box 969
Wheaton, IL 60187

World Christian (an independent, evangelical magazine created to challenge, encourage and equip Christians who have a heart for the world)
P.O. Box 40010
Pasadena, CA 91104

World Evangelization
Lausanne Committee of World Evangelization
P.O. Box 1100
Wheaton, Il 60189

World Vision Magazine and International Intercessor
World Vision International
919 W. Huntington Drive
Monrovia, CA 91109

World Wide Challenge
Campus Crusade for Christ
Arrowhead Springs
San Bernardino, CA 92401

Worldwide News
Pocket Testament League
117 Main Street
Lincoln Park, NJ 07035

Worldwide Thrust
Worldwide Evangelization Crusade
P.O. Box A
Fort Washington, PA 19034

The Zwemer Institute Newsletter (to reach unreached
Muslims for Christ)
Zwemer Institute
Box 365
Altadena, CA 91001

NOTE: For $32.50 a year the *Evangelical Missions Information Service* provides the following vision-building materials:

Missions News Service - a bi-monthly update on current activities in the whole world of missions

Pulse - a periodical in-depth study of missions in key regions of the world, such as Asia, Latin America, Africa, Europe, etc.

Evangelical Missions Quarterly - news and hard-hitting articles on mission trends and challenges today.

To subscribe, write to: Evangelical Missions Information Services, Box 794, Wheaton, IL 60187

Magazines from Some Denominations with Large Missionary Forces

Alliance Witness
Christian & Missionary Alliance
Overseas Ministries
P.O. Box C
Nyack, NY 10960

Call to Prayer (monthly)
Assemblies of God
Division of Foreign Missions
1445 Boonville Avenue
Springfield, MO 65802

Commission
Southern Baptist Convention
Foreign Mission Board
Box 5697
Richmond, VA 23230

Impact
Conservative Baptist Foreign Missions Society
Wheaton, IL 60187

Secular Magazines with a World Perspective

Aboriginal Identity
Aboriginal Publications Foundation
Box M931, G.P.O.
Perth, W.A. 6000
AUSTRALIA

Africa (An international business, economic and political monthly)
Africa Journal Ltd.
Kerkman House, 54a Tottenham Ct. Rd.
London W1P 0BT
ENGLAND

Africa News (a weekly newspaper)
P.O. Box 3851
Durham, NC 27702

African Directions
884 National Press Bldg.
Washington, DC 20045

Americas (The Inter-American Magazine)
Subscription Service Dept.
P.O. Box 973
Farmingdale, NY 11737

Amnesty International Newsletter
10 Southampton St.
London WC2E 7HF
ENGLAND

Aramco World Magazine (The world of the Middle East)
1345 Avenue of the Americas
New York, NY 10019

Asia World
Chatterjie International Centre
33-A Chowringhee Rd.
Calcutta 700 071
INDIA

Asian Outlook
1 Tsingtao East Rd.
Taipei
REPUBLIC OF CHINA

Atlas: World Press Review; News and Views from the
Foreign Press
Box 915
Farmingdale, NY 11737

China Now (for Anglo-Chinese understanding)
152 Camden High St.
London, NW1 0NE
ENGLAND

Christian Science Monitor
One Norway Street
Boston, MA 02115

Far Eastern Economic Review
G.P.O. Box 160
HONG KONG

The Futurist (a journal about global forecasts, trends and ideas about the future)
World Future Society
P.O. Box 30369, Bethesda Branch
Washington, DC 20014

Latin American Weekly Report
Latin American Newsletter Ltd.
90-93 Cowcross St.
London EC1M 6BC
ENGLAND

The Link: American for Middle East Understanding
Room 771, 475 Riverside Dr.
New York, NY 10027

Media Today
Living Media India Ltd.
9 K-Block, Connaught Circus
New Delhi 110 021
INDIA

MEED (Middle East Economic Digest)
MABCO, Inc., 61 Broadway
New York, NY 10006

National Geographic
17th & M Streets NW
Washington, DC 20036

New York Times
2229 W. 43rd Street
New York, NY 10036

Pacific Islands Monthly
2812 Kahawai Street
Honolulu, HI 96822

Pacific Research
Pacific Studies Center
Mountain View, CA 94041

The Rotarian
1600 Ridge Ave.
Evanston, IL 60201

The Southeast Asia Record
Asia-Pacific Affairs Association
580 College Ave., Suite 6
Palo Alto, CA 94306

Soviet Life
Embassy of the USSR
1706-18th St., NW
Washington, DC 20009

Travel
Travel Building
Floral Park, NY 11001

U.S. News and World Report
Subscription Department
P.O. Box 2627,
Boulder, CO 80321

Wall Street Journal
Dow Jones Co., Inc.
22 Cortlandt Street
New York, NY 10007

World Development
Pergarnon Press, Inc.
Maxwell House, Fairview Park
Elmsford, NY 10524

World Issues
Center for the Study of
Democratic Institutions
2056 Eucalyptus Hill Road
Santa Barbara, CA 93108

World Student News
International Union of Students
17th November St., 11001 Prague 01
CZECHOSLOVAKIA

The World Today
Royal Institute of International Affa
Chatham House, 10 St. James Squar
London SW1X 4LE
ENGLAND

Worldview
P.O. Box 1308M
Fort Lee, NY 07024

Magazines That Move: Mission Films

The following are just a few of the resources available to you for slide/tape and film presentations on world missions. Contact each organization for full information on what they offer and their rental fees (if any). When you write, be sure to specify your audience and request information on the charges to you.

Africa Inland Mission
Box 178
Pearl River, NY 10965

Conservative Baptist Foreign Missions Society
Box 5
Wheaton, IL 60187

Gospel Films
Box 455
Muskegon, MI 49443

International Films, Inc.
1605 E. Elizabeth
Pasadena, CA 91104

Ken Anderson Films
Box 618
Winona Lake, IN 46590

Overseas Crusade
Box 66
Santa Clara, CA 95050

Overseas Missionary Fellowship
404 South Church Street
Robesonia, PA 19551

Team Films
Box 969
Wheaton, IL 60187

Twenty-One Hundred Productions
233 Langdon
Madison, WI 53703

Worldwide Evangelization Crusade
Box A
Fort Washington, PA 19034

Organizations

Association of Christian Ministries to Internationals
233 Langdon
Madison, WI 53703
Note: A cooperative effort of more than 20 groups seeking to reach international visitors to the U.S.

Association of Church Missions Committees
1620 S. Myrtle Ave.   P.O. Box ACMC
Monrovia, CA 91016   Wheaton, IL 60187
Note: Their motto is "Churches Helping Churches in Missions"
Offers:
> Training conferences for churches at the local level
> National conferences
> Missions Resource Center
> Missions Policy Handbook
> Missions Education Handbook
> ...plus other helpful literature and consulting services
> for the local church

Campus Crusade for Christ
Arrowhead Springs
San Bernardino, CA 92404
Offers:
> International Resources Office
> Agape Movement (vocational witness overseas)
> STOP OUT! Program (1 year overseas)

International Summer Projects
World Wide Challenge magazine
Here's Life World! campaign
Specialists on international student ministry
Staff openings in over 100 countries outside USA

Christian Nationals Evangelism Commission
1470 N. Fourth St.
San Jose, CA 95112
Note: Opportunities to give support ministry to established indigenous evangelistic work in 35 nations.

Evangelicals for Social Action
P.O. Box 76560
Washington, DC 20013
Offers:

> World Peace Projects
> Workshops on Discipleship and International Justice
> Public Policy Task Forces (such as urban concerns)
> Updates on a variety of issues that directly or indirectly impinge on world evangelization

Evangelical Foreign Missions Association (EFMA)
1430 K Street NW
Washington, DC 20005
Note: Involving both denominational and non-denominational societies, it is the mission affiliate of the National Association of Evangelicals.
Offers:

> *Missionary News Service* (semi-monthly)
> *Evangelical Missions Quarterly*

Evangelical Missions Information Service
Box 794
Wheaton, IL 60187
Offers:

> *Evangelical Missions Quarterly*
> *Missionary News Service*
> Pulses (Africa, Asia, Europe, Latin America, Chinese World, Muslim World)

Global Church Growth Book Club
1705 Sierra Bonita Ave.
Pasadena, CA 91104
Offers: A special selection of books (discounted) suited to those exploring the World Christian theme. Also, the major outlet for hundreds of titles published by William Carey Library.

Gospel Light Publications
2300 Knoll Dr.
Ventura, CA 93003
Offers: Regal Books (ask for their catalog and a listing of their titles on world missions)

Interdenominational Foreign Missions Association (IFMA)
Box 395
Wheaton, IL 60187
Note: an association of evangelical foreign mission societies without denominational affiliation.
Offers:
>   *Missionary News Service* (semi-monthly)
>   *Evangelical Missions Quarterly*

International Fellowship of Evangelical Students
P.O. Box 270
Madison, WI 53701

International Students Incorporated
Box C
Colorado Springs, CO 80901
Offers:
>   Literature both for training and evangelism with
>   foreign students
>   Training conferences
>   Staff nationwide

Inter-Varsity Missions
233 Langdon St.
Madison, WI 53703

Offers:

> World Christian Handbooks Series
> World Christian Conferences
> World Christian Video Training Curriculum
> Student Training in Missions
> Overseas Training Camps
> World Missions Training Camp, USA
> URBANA Student Missions Convention
> Mission Specialists nationwide
> Christmas House Parties for international students
> Student Foreign Missions Fellowship

Inter-Varsity Press
Downers Grove, IL 60515
Note: Ask for their latest catalog and a listing of their titles on world missions.

Lausanne Committee for World Evangelization
Whitefield House
186 Kennington Park Rd.
London SE11 4BT
England
Note: An international network to alert Christians to the needs and opportunities in world evangelization and to foster cooperative efforts to that end among the worldwide evangelical community. Publishes monthly the World Evangelization Information News Service, free upon request.

National Prayer Committee
P.O. Box 6826
San Bernardino, CA 92412
Note: An interdenominational effort of recognized prayer leaders to mobilize prayer in the Church, nationally and locally, for spiritual awakening and world evangelization.
Offers:

> Training materials
> Conferences
> Consultations
> ...and other services

Navigators
P.O. Box 1659
Colorado Springs, CO 80901
Note: Involved in 34 countries, the Navs offer opportunities to students who have been helped first in their specialized training programs. *Nav Log* highlights their work around the world.

U.S.Center for World Mission
1605 E. Elizabeth St.
Pasadena, CA 91104
Includes:
>   Institute for Chinese Studies
>   Institute for Muslim Studies
>   Institute for Hindu Studies
>   Institute for Tribal Studies
>   Order for World Evangelization
>   Fellowship of World Christians
>   Oversees Counseling Service
>   Frontier Fellowship

World Evangelical Fellowship
Wheaton, IL 60187
Note: An association of national evangelical fellowships, committed to mutual support and exchange in fulfilling the task of world evangelization. Publishes a quarterly bulletin *Global Report*, free on request.

World Relief Commission
P.O. Box WRC
Wheaton, IL 60187
Note: One of many fine organizations that provides meaningful ways to minister to physical needs in Christ's name.

World Vision International/Missions Advanced Research and Communication Center (MARC)
919 West Huntington Dr.
Monrovia, CA 91016